T0375918

WHAT YOUR COLLEAGUES ARE SAYIN

Leader Ready gets to the root of what is holding back aspiring leaders from pursuing the role of principal and provides a blueprint for supporting our future leaders. Cusack and Bustamante draw from their many years in leadership to bring us this great advice. *Leader Ready* is a must for every principal's bookshelf!

Carmen Markowski
Assistant Principal, St. Joseph Catholic School
Spruce Grove, Alberta, Canada

We owe emerging school leaders the conditions, strategies, and opportunities necessary to grow and succeed. Cusack and Bustamante's work is a major step forward in the right direction!

Wayne Davies
Vice Principal, Nelson McIntyre Collegiate Institute
East St. Paul, Manitoba, Canada

Leader Ready is a must-have resource for anyone supporting the development of aspiring leaders. Cusack and Bustamante's Universal Leadership Standards, leadership development model, and templates provide a road map for building leadership capacity.

Kelli Leavell
Author, Consultant, and District Coordinator, Bremerton School District
Bremerton, Washington

Any leader at any stage in their career can gain something from this book. Cusack and Bustamante's Universal Leadership Standards provide a framework that can be utilized by even the most seasoned educational leaders for years to come!

Ryan Persaud
Educational Leader, The International School of Curitiba
Curitiba, Brazil

Cusack and Bustamante provide us with a vision for inspiring the most opportune yet underserved school leaders: assistant principals. The authors' focus on informed and strategic professional growth encourages aspiring leaders to engage with the challenges of today's school systems with confidence and wisdom.

Sam Jordan
Grant Director, Alaska Council of School Administrators
Juneau, Alaska

This book will develop great principals who support assistant principals to become great future principals. Cusack and Bustamante deliver a path to connect potential and intention and move to dynamic implementation. Their interactive approach is rooted in standards and supported by lived experience.

Randy Hetherington
Associate Professor of Educational Leadership, University of Portland
Portland, Oregon

This book offers practical strategies and tools for developing leadership skills in aspiring and novice school and district leaders. Cusack and Bustamante synthesize the research and issues relevant to assistant principals differentiated by level of experience, something rarely accomplished.

Andrea Kane
Professor of Practice in Educational Leadership
University of Pennsylvania Graduate School of Education
Philadelphia, Pennsylvania

LEADER READY

LEADER READY

Four Pathways to Prepare Aspiring School Leaders

TIM CUSACK

VINCE BUSTAMANTE

FOREWORD BY PETER DEWITT
AFTERWORD BY JOHN HATTIE

A SAGE Publishing Company

For information:

Corwin
A SAGE Company
2455 Teller Road
Thousand Oaks, California 91320
(800) 233-9936
www.corwin.com

SAGE Publications Ltd.
1 Oliver's Yard
55 City Road
London EC1Y 1SP
United Kingdom

SAGE Publications India Pvt. Ltd.
Unit No 323-333, Third Floor, F-Block
International Trade Tower Nehru Place
New Delhi 110 019
India

SAGE Publications Asia-Pacific Pte. Ltd.
18 Cross Street #10-10/11/12
China Square Central
Singapore 048423

ISBN 978-1-0719-1679-7

This book is printed on acid-free paper.

Vice President and Editorial Director:
  Monica Eckman
Senior Acquisitions Editor: Tanya Ghans
Content Development Manager:
  Desirée A. Bartlett
Senior Editorial Assistant: Nyle De Leon
Production Editor: Vijayakumar
Copy Editor: Christobel Colleen Hopman
Typesetter: TNQ Technologies
Proofreader: Benny Willy Stephen
Indexer: TNQ Technologies
Cover Designer: Scott Van Atta
Marketing Manager: Morgan Fox

23 24 25 26 27 10 9 8 7 6 5 4 3 2 1

CONTENTS

Foreword by Peter DeWitt   ix

Acknowledgments   xi

Publisher's Acknowledgments   xiii

About the Authors   xv

Your Guide to This Book   xvii

1. An Answer to Leadership in Crisis   1
     The Great Resignation   2
     The Great Opt Out   3
     Barriers to Leadership   4
     Always Stuck in Second Gear   6
     A New Metaphor for Growth and Development   7
     Four Roots of School Leader Preparation   10
     Predictive Inquiry   14

2. Raising the Bar on Leadership Standards   15
     What Do Leadership Standards Do for Us?   17
     Standards Around the World   20
     Using Universal Leadership Standards to Inform Training   23
     Implementation Points to Ponder   30
     Predictive Inquiry   31

3. Creating a Culture for Implementation   33
     What Is a Culture for Implementation?   35
     Measuring Self-Efficacy   46
     Unpacking Cusack's (2020) Findings   47
     The Culture for Implementation   49
     Implementation Points to Ponder   50
     Predictive Inquiry   52

4. Planning Guided Leadership Experiences   53

    What Do We Know About Guided Experience?   54

    Progressions of Experiences   55

    Moving From Guided to Mastery Learning Experiences   58

    Samples of Level of Experiences Aligned With Universal
      Leadership Standards   62

    Leadership Development and Trust   68

    Guided Leadership Experiences   73

    Implementation Points to Ponder   73

    Predictive Inquiry   74

5. Attaining Mastery Experiences   75

    What Mastery Means   76

    What the Research Says About Mastery Experience   78

    What Does Mastery at Level 3 Look Like?   87

    Celebrating Mastery   95

    Ways to Celebrate Mastery Milestones   96

    Moving the Level 3 Assistant Principal Onto the Pathway   97

    Implementation Points to Ponder   99

    Predictive Inquiry   100

Conclusion: Implementing the Four Roots—Our Perspectives   101

Afterword by John Hattie   105

Appendices   109

    Appendix 1: Research on the Self-Efficacy of Assistant
      Principals   110

    Appendix 2: Comparing Leadership Standards   112

    Appendix 3: Universal Leadership Standard (ULS) Inventory   113

    Appendix 4: Levels of Experience Template   123

    Appendix 5: Feedback Template for Skill, Will, and Thrill   124

    Appendix 6: Culminating Activity: Leadership Growth Plan
      Template   125

References   133

Index   139

Visit **https://us.corwin.com/books/
leader-ready-281684**
for downloadable resources.

FOREWORD

For eight years I was fortunate enough to be a principal of a school in upstate, New York. I entered the principalship without any experience. However, the panel of 17 people, which included teachers, parents, and leaders, chose me based on potential and the fact that I had 11 years of teaching experience in several high poverty city schools.

Over the years I was a principal, I had great support from the leaders in the district office, my leadership colleagues from the other schools in our district, but more importantly from the teachers, students, and community I served.

As I entered the world of leadership consulting, I quickly found that not all leaders were fortunate enough to have the support that I did so long ago. In fact, I remember running a series of workshops for the University of Oklahoma for assistant principals. Our focus was on instructional leadership. As I went through the different facets of my instructional leadership work, I could tell that something was wrong. It was not the content. Instead, it was the barriers they felt to do the work. In a survey of the 26 people in the room, the number one barrier to practicing instructional leadership as an assistant principal was their principal.

Since I was not an assistant principal and did not have one when I was a principal, it never occurred to me that the principal, the person who was supposed to be the mentor of the assistant principal, could be a barrier.

In all fairness, it was not always due to the principal not wanting to be a mentor to show the assistant principal how to practice instructional leadership. There were times when the principal didn't know how to practice it either, or it was due to the school needing all hands-on deck, so the assistant principal spent their time doing discipline.

The issue is also due to out-of-date university preparatory programs that often focus too much of their time and effort on management, and not enough on instructional leadership, student and teacher engagement, and collaboration.

This cycle needs to end. The cycle I am referring to is when principals "train" assistant principals the same way those principals were "trained" when they were assistants. Too often I work with assistant principals who are frustrated because they want to be a leader but too often must spend most of their time patrolling hallways and disciplining students for offenses that are too many to count due to our students' lives becoming more complicated as well.

This all matters for very practical reasons. No matter where you are in the world, if you are a leader you need to formally observe your teachers. If you do not get into classrooms, talk with students and teachers about learning, and learn along with your teachers, you will lack credibility in your role. And that means that the feedback you try to offer teachers will fall flat because they will most likely not see you or your feedback as credible.

However, there is something else which is just as important. Connection. When adults in the school do not feel connected to their school, there is a higher level of anxiety and depression. Without connecting as a school community there will be a good chance our schools will lack an identity. We become individuals who have forgotten why we entered education in the first place.

This is where Tim Cusack and Vince Bustamante come into the picture. I met Vince a few years ago, when I was speaking in Saskatoon, Canada, and we quickly bonded. I met Tim a few months later when I was working in their district. The two of them had an impactful partnership, and their focus on growing leaders, especially those in the assistant principal role, was inspiring.

This book is a guide to help assistant principals see a world that they can help create. Those that feel like victims of their own circumstances will find some light to focus on. As leaders and potential leaders reading this book, you will find standards, stories, a framework, and strategies that you can grab onto and try out. You will learn about the importance of implementation and hear stories from the field— from people who have been in your shoes and understand what it's like to be where you are.

However, this book is not just a guide but a connection. I know Tim and Vince. Their words ring out and I can hear their voices as I read them. They know how to develop connections, provide hope (and we all need hope), and help you find the strategies you need to use as you move forward.

Many years ago, when I was a teacher, my principal spoke to me about going back to get my master's degree in school administration. In the middle of our hallway, I said no way. I would never be a principal. What changed my mind was two retired teachers who I knew from my gym. They asked me, "What if you could be the principal you want to be, and not the one you have to be?"

Don't just read Tim and Vince's guidance, research, and strategies through the eyes of what is, but try to read them through the lens of what could be. Find your entry point and move forward.

—Peter DeWitt, EdD

ACKNOWLEDGMENTS

From Tim Cusack:

The journey of a thousand miles begins with a single step.
                                                    –Lao Tzu

The journey along *Leader Ready* has been so incredibly humbling and rewarding. It has been such a rich learning opportunity for me, one which has empowered me to put research into action! My first step that whisked me into this adventure was to acknowledge the incredibly important role and work of assistant principals. In many ways they are our unsung heroes, and this book is dedicated to them with the true desire and hope to shine more light on their pathway and to honor and celebrate their leadership. We need them to be our next generation of principals and to enter the role with confidence and courage.

In terms of thanks and appreciation, I begin with my dear colleague. Vince has helped me understand better how aspiring leaders can be empowered to take risks and reach new levels of professional learning when given authentic and meaningful voice in the conversation. Writing this book leveraged his previous experiences as an author and he, in so many ways, guided me along this pathway. I also want to thank Ariel Curry and Peter DeWitt whose encouragement to share the need to do more for our assistant principals motivated me to step forward. They connected me with amazing Tanya Ghans and wonderful Wendy Murray, both of whom have made this experience of writing such a dynamic and powerful experience. I have so many great memories working with Vince and Wendy from the many different places we worked from to get this book to fruition. Whether St. Pete Beach, Edmonton, Calgary, Hawaii, Alaska, California, Antigua, Bahamas, New Brunswick…, wherever we each happened to be, we persevered and what you see before you is the fruit of that labor.

I extend deep thanks to my colleagues in Edmonton Catholic Schools for their support of this important work. Also, a debt of gratitude is offered to all who reviewed the book and lent their voice to the greater conversation of doing more to support our assistant principals' professional growth and development.

Finally, I thank my wife, Susan, and my family for their unwavering support and encouragement as I walked along the pathway to see this book to fruition.

From Vince Bustamante:

I am so thankful to be able to coauthor this timely book with my dear friend, colleague, and mentor, Dr. Tim Cusack. Thank you for the sage advice you continue to impart on me every conversation we have. From the beginning stages when you were my principal to collaborating on this project together, I am so grateful to learn from you. I am very excited to see where we go next along the pathway.

This book would not have been possible without the contributions of some of the stellar leaders I have been lucky to meet and work alongside. Thank you, Ryan, Toni, Wayne, and Nicole for adding your voice and perspectives to the text. I am also so thankful to all of our peer reviewers for their perspectives and suggestions.

Thank you to the brilliant editorial team at Corwin, Tanya Ghans and Wendy Murray. This book would not have been possible without you, you are as much a part of this as we are. A special thank you to Ariel Curry for sparking this idea in us and helping us out in the planning stage. I have been extremely fortunate to have Peter DeWitt as a mentor and sounding board throughout this and many other projects. Thank you, Peter, for the facetime chats, advice, and ideas as I navigated my way through this project.

Finally, and most importantly, I would like to thank my wife Leah for her support as I finished book project #3. Throughout this process, we relocated cities, changed career paths, and welcomed our first child into the world, baby Luca. To say it has been a whirlwind would be an understatement, and I am so thankful for your partnership, support, and encouragement. Our growing family is so lucky to have you.

PUBLISHER'S ACKNOWLEDGMENTS

Corwin gratefully acknowledges the contributions of the following reviewers:

Jennifer Allen, Principal
Highlands Junior High School
Edmonton, Canada

Ken Darvall, Principal
Tema International School
Tema, Ghana

Angela M. Molsey, Adjunct Professor
Brightpoint Community College
Chester, Virginia

Cathy Patterson, Retired Elementary Educator
Diamond Bar, California

Lena Marie Rockwood, Assistant Principal for Student Success
Revere High School
Revere, Massachusetts

Catherine Sosnowski, Adjunct Professor
Central Connecticut State University
New Britain, Connecticut

ABOUT THE AUTHORS

Tim Cusack, EdD, is an educator with 30 years of experience as a classroom teacher, department head, assistant principal, principal, assistant superintendent of learning services (curriculum, assessment, professional development), and currently serves as deputy superintendent of Edmonton Catholic Schools (Leadership Support Services). In his current role, he directly supports the daily work of school leadership teams and aspiring leaders across almost 100 schools.

Tim is passionate about leadership development, mentorship, and systems change and improvement. His doctoral work through the University of Portland centered upon the self-efficacy of assistant principals and how to better prepare them for principalship.

Additionally, Tim has over 30 years of experience as a Naval Warfare Officer with the Royal Canadian Navy (Reserve) including four years as executive officer and three years as commanding officer of HMCS NONSUCH in Edmonton. Tim has delivered many presentations and keynote addresses across Canada and in the United States. This book is his first with Corwin. He can be found on Twitter: @CusackTim and at www.timothycusack.com.

Vince Bustamante, MEd, is an instructional coach, curriculum content developer, and author who resides in Calgary, Canada. He is the coauthor of two bestselling books with Corwin: *Great Teaching by Design* and *The Assessment Playbook for Distance and Blended Learning*. Vince is passionate about implementation, assessment, and creating classroom environments that foster deep learning experiences where teachers understand and evaluate their impact. He specializes in working with teachers, leadership teams, schools, and school districts as they seek to implement high-impact strategies and systems for school improvement. He can be found on Twitter: @Vincebusta and at www.vincebustamante.com.

YOUR GUIDE
TO THIS BOOK

THE COMBINED EXPERIENCE BEHIND THIS BOOK

When you pick up a book by any author, whether thriller writer, pop psychologist, or economist, you want to know their street cred, right? What's their expertise? Agenda? And perhaps most importantly, what drove them to drop everything in their busy lives to do the insanely hard work of writing a book? With *Leader Ready: Four Pathways to Prepare Aspiring School Leaders*, you get to peek into the backgrounds of not one, but two lives. First and foremost, we are professional colleagues and friends. We live in Canada, and as you will see, we like trees, and we like walking among them. That's an inside joke, but by the end of Chapter 1, you will be in on it.

COAUTHOR COLLABORATION

It was 2013 when I (Tim) first met Vince. I was serving as a principal of a junior/senior high school and Vince was serving as a teacher in our Social Studies Department. His instruction and assessment practices were stellar, and it was not long afterward that Vince assumed the role of Department Head (Social Studies). We collaborated on numerous school and jurisdictional improvement projects and shared our work at professional learning workshops and conferences. In 2015, when I assumed the role as assistant-superintendent of Learning Services (Curriculum, Assessment, Professional Learning), we brought Vince onboard to assume a divisional leadership role as a consultant (Social Studies and Assessment). We deepened shared interest in teacher and leader self-efficacy and collaborated on further projects. Our work served as inspiration for each of us to pursue doctoral studies.

Tim: A District Leader's Perspective

In 2020, I was appointed as Deputy Chief Superintendent, and a big part of my assigned duties included the identification, hiring, and training of principals and assistant principals. I soon discovered that over 50% of our current principals could retire imminently, so when I did doctoral research at University of Portland, I focused my attention on learning and leadership. I wanted to understand how we, as a division, might attract more assistant principals to follow the pathway to principalship. The findings suggested that our existing formation programming, while well received, was not enough to move the hearts and minds of the undecided forward. Too many talented folks were opting out. My doctoral work sought to answer why—exactly—this was so, and what professional learning experiences could we design to keep them engaged. That research informs our work going forward and we are excited to share our insights with you.

Vince: A Divisional Leader Perspective

Leadership can take many forms. For me it has always been instructional in focus. After being in the classroom for a few years, I found myself in the role of a department head. I became acquainted with the variety of leadership roles that exist in a school, but I knew I could use my responsibility to lead my department to better serve students. My responsibilities turned to serving our district in the form of a Curriculum Consultant. Being solely responsible for curriculum implementation, development, and consistency in social studies across our district led me to seek out more leadership experiences. Learning to become a better leader became a necessity to me, as I wanted to ensure the path I was creating for myself was forged in research. This led me to connect with some of the brightest minds in education and through that I was able to coauthor two noteworthy education books, with the minds of John Hattie, John Almarode, Doug Fisher, and Nancy Frey. Through this experience, I now spend my time working internationally with districts to assist them in the implementation and evaluation of instructional practices.

WHO IS THIS BOOK FOR?

The overall purpose of this book is to engage in a process of learning, conversation, action, and implementation of our new model of leadership development. Here is how we see professionals using it.

> *District Leaders:* Professionals at this level are usually tasked with implementing principal training in a district. Our book is aimed first and foremost at this audience because we are after systemwide improvement. We provide a research-based model for training that can "plug and play" in any school setting, and in each chapter provide research data, implementation ideas, and insights on the planning and pacing of ongoing mentoring. We strongly believe that even though district leaders by necessity must stay at the "big picture" level of leadership, when they are handed a resource like *Leader Ready: Four Pathways to Prepare Aspiring School Leaders,* they are able to get down to the ground level of a principal's daily work and effect change The leadership development model in this book allows them to support principals' growth as mentors to rising talent in their ranks.

Principals: What book author *wouldn't* want multiple audiences for their work? We recognize that principals work in a constant "putting out fires" mentality and can be so strapped for time they don't think they can pause and learn. We've both been in those roles. Nevertheless, we have written this resource so it's practical enough and yet systematic enough to help principals jump in and "do." Whether a principal wishes to launch an ambitious new training initiative in the school or just dip in and out and try the ideas in this book, we trust it will become a well-worn, dog-eared resource.

Assistant Principals: These are the educators we are trying to rescue, frankly. Assistant principals are the leaders of tomorrow, and too many of them are working without sufficient support. This book is intended to give current assistant (vice) principals appropriate insights into how to best prepare to assume the role of principal.

Department Heads, Coaches, and Others: Last but certainly not least, this book is for all those who are responsible for the identification and development of leaders in a school. At heart the book shows every educator how to develop self-efficacy, within themselves and in others. By going further upstream, so to speak, we can encourage our teacher leaders to consider stepping onto the pathway to formal school leadership.

FEATURES OF THIS BOOK

This book is designed to support the professional learning and development of individual leaders as well as leadership teams. As such, we have included the following features in each chapter to give you some tools for inquiry and discussions.

Universal Leadership Standards: Each chapter will highlight key leadership standards that will be the foundation for the theory and practice of the chapter. After analyzing leadership standards from multiple countries, states, and provinces, we have highlighted what we feel are the most important ones to the development of assistant principals.

Voices From the Field: Each chapter will have examples of leaders from across the globe who will share their insights and explanations as it pertains to the development of assistant principals in their respective areas of expertise.

Activities: Through the book you will find activities that will help you reflect on and process the information presented in the book.

Rooted Reflections: These prompts provide a focus for discussion and reflection.

Systems Checks: These invite the reader to consider and reflect upon existing practices and structures within their organization. Using an evaluative approach, consider how our recommendations may differ from existing realities in your organization.

Implementation Points to Ponder: If you are responsible for actionable professional learning opportunities, consider starting as you plan for meetings and professional learning sessions for leaders.

PUTTING IT ALL TOGETHER

This book fills a necessary gap in the formation of school leaders and provides a clear and practical approach to the mentorship and development of the aspiring school leader. Assistant (or vice) principals, department heads, lead teachers, instructional coaches, and all other teacher leaders in your school will find this content relevant, rigorous, and useful. By acknowledging the obvious gap in research and the ever increasing need to attract more people to school based leadership, our framework seeks to develop all those who aspire to become leaders in their schools and school districts. Principals and district leaders alike will find the content of this book useful to support the development of leaders in their localized contexts. We recognize there is a crisis in educational leadership development. Our framework seeks to provide strategies to mitigate the complex and challenging issues faced by schools and school districts.

CHAPTER 1

························

AN ANSWER TO LEADERSHIP IN CRISIS

Twenty years from now you will be more disappointed by the things you didn't do than by the ones you did do. So throw off the bowlines. Sail away from the safe harbor. Catch the trade winds in your sails. Explore. Dream. Discover.

—Mark Twain

Source: iStock.com/Nicola Katie

Let's begin by imagining a hundred assistant principals (APs) gathered in a meeting room. About one-fifth of them are veterans of 10 or more years, a third are within the 4–9 years range of experience, and the majority are within their first three years of formal school-based leadership. If we asked how many of them aspire to become a principal, how many would say yes? How many would say no? How many might be undecided? What reasons might they cite for persevering to principalship? What would they say undercut their desire to continue?

FIGURE 1.1   ASSISTANT PRINCIPALS: HOW MANY ASPIRE TO BE PRINCIPALS?

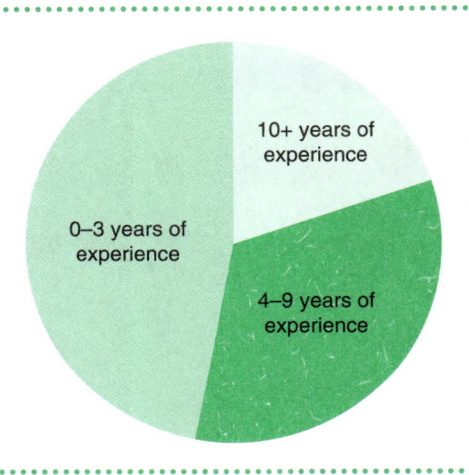

If you are reading this book, chances are you have a good grasp of how the responses would go, and the picture isn't a rosy one. But we wrote this resource because we believe there can be a bright future—if we heed the research and create better conditions for our aspiring leaders. The framework we will share with you will ask you to sail away from the safe harbor—all that is familiar and known—in favor of exploring new ideas and new possibilities that can improve aspiring leader mentoring and development and entice more of them to consider principalship. In this book, we show you how to work with principals throughout the school year to achieve systemic professional growth. So, let's throw off the bowlines, sail away from the safe harbor, and catch the trade winds in our sails as we start off by exploring the urgency of the current situation.

THE GREAT RESIGNATION

The "great resignation" is a phenomenon that has gained attention in the past few years. The pandemic and the measures taken to contain it caused people to reassess their lives. The what, when, and where of work and career has changed. In education, I (Tim) have observed that we are also witnessing the "great retirement." Historically, principals have tended to serve a few years beyond the threshold of years or age set by the state. This is no longer the case. More people who can retire "on time" do so. Thus, many seasoned principals are retiring sooner than we might normally experience. In my school division, about 50% of the principals are at retirement eligibility, and I suspect the numbers are similar where you work. There is great urgency to encourage APs to aspire for principalship.

We are at a crossroads, if not a crisis, in terms of principal succession planning and succession management. Given the increased instances of resignation, early retirement, and burnout, many school jurisdictions are backed into a corner when it comes to staffing. They are forced to place people with less diverse experience and commensurate leadership training into roles requiring greater levels of responsibility and higher levels of complexity. This is not a winning combination, for it makes all involved at risk of faltering and dropping out.

Studies conducted over the past decade suggest the attrition of school principals is approaching unprecedented levels. In 2019, the National Association of Secondary School Principals (NASSP) and the Learning Policy Institute (LPI) studied several factors that lead to principal turnover (attrition) and found that 42% of survey respondents ($N = 424$) and 33 school leaders from 26 states planned to leave their current school or the principalship outright based on such factors as working conditions, compensation, accountability systems, decision-making authority, and professional learning (Levin, Scott, Yang, Leung, & Bradley, 2020). In this introductory chapter, we delve into attrition and research on other factors compromising school leadership; for now, it's enough to know that the well is running dry.

THE GREAT OPT OUT

"The great opt out" of APs is the second stressor. These young, talented educators are looking at the increasing complexity, challenge, and workload of principals and thinking, *well, maybe not*. When I (Tim) canvassed my current cadre of APs about their disposition toward becoming a principal, well over 40% were uncertain if they wanted to follow the path to that next leadership destination. Why?

For one thing, the role itself is highly complex. APs are often tasked with wearing many hats in a school. The tasks often seem menial and repetitive. What's more, the responsibilities vary from school to school, so the AP can't look to a consistent standard or lean on clear benchmarks. Research in the past decades reminds us that the function of the AP role is important but chronically ill-defined. For better or for worse, APs are at the whim of the principal they support. As one AP commented, "assistant principals are like school-based porters rather than principals in training."

Along with this all too apt porter comparison, APs are burdened by uneven, sometimes inadequate, training. Sure, there are always those individuals who will become successful principals despite the obstacles, but the statistics show too many potentially effective leaders decide not to persevere to principalship due to poor support. Feelings of unpreparedness combined with the unpredictability of the job are preventing great people from becoming great principals.

BARRIERS TO LEADERSHIP

Research also shows that in addition to resignations and opting out, many social, cultural, economic, religious, and gender identity barriers exist for those who may want to seek leadership opportunities. In her study, *Pathways to the Superintendency: The Experiences of Albertan Female Superintendents*, Dr. Susan Coates (2020) observed, "Currently, the incidence of women serving in the role of Superintendent of Schools in Alberta is disproportionate to the 74% female educators serving as teachers (Alberta Teacher Retirement Fund, 2017) and 45% of women serving as principals" (Alberta Education, 2013). These findings suggest the issue that may exist is not the lack of capable leaders rather the harsh environmental conditions conducive to a lack of female representation. "Given the shared standards of professional practice among these three groups of educators (teachers, principals, superintendents), there is a demographic discrepancy that is mathematically disproportionate between the representation of women serving as teachers compared to those serving as [principals and] Superintendent of Schools" (Coates, 2020). It is clear that there is a need for more proportional representation in our school leaders.

Although research from the last 50 years reinforces the importance that APs play in school improvement, it is well known that preparation, leadership training, and programs are inconsistent. It is true that some districts do a good job at providing training modules, professional learning, and courses but in many cases AP mentorship is simply left to chance. We know there are great leadership preparation programs scattered across districts, but we struggle with the lack of deliberate focus for aspiring leaders. There is simply too much theory and not enough practical application. APs have been clear in their desire to experience hands-on, deliberate, and focused preparation so that they are prepared to take on the role of principal.

Our goal with this book is to look head on at how leaders can support the formation, development, and growth of APs. We focus on APs because the research tells us that this group of school leaders has been "one of the least researched and least discussed topics in educational leadership" (Weller &Weller, 2002, p. xiii) for the past 50 years. Wait what?! Fifty years? If you think that does not sound quite right, let's take a look at some of the key ideas stemming from each of the past five decades (Figure 1.2).

FIGURE 1.2 SUMMARY OF RESEARCH ON ASSISTANT PRINCIPALS

DECADE OF RESEARCH	KEY FINDINGS
1970s Austin and Brown (1970)	• The work of an AP is largely managerial and menial. • The dynamic between AP and principal is important, but inconsistent in terms of preparation. • *More should be done to develop this important group of leaders.*
1980s Reed and Himler (1985) Fulton (1987) Marshall and Greenfield (1987)	• Existing research suggested the role of AP is yet to be conceptualized. • APs are disadvantaged in the area of instructional research; this domain must be developed. • The role needs to be clearly defined. • *More should be done to develop this important group of leaders.*
1990s Marshall (1993) Scroggins and Bishop (1993) Hartzell (1993a) Glanz (1994)	• Role of AP largely revolved around managing students, scheduling, cocurricular activities, and staff supervision. • Scope of their work was largely determined by the principal. • Work assigned was too managerial and not instructionally focused. • *More should be done to develop this important group of leaders.*
2000s Weller and Weller (2002) Davis, Darling-Hammond, Meyerson, and LaPointe (2005) Villani (2006) Darling-Hammond (2007) Armstrong (2005, 2009)	• Although much is stated of what should be done, little is suggested in terms of how to better develop and nurture the self-efficacy of school leaders. • Inadequate training, poor placement and induction methodologies, lack of effective communication, and ineffective feedback mechanisms contributes to job strain. • *More should be done to develop this important group of leaders.*
2010s Armstrong (2010) Barnett, Shoho, and Oleszewski (2012) Lehman, Boyland, and Sriver (2014) Murphy (2017) Searby, Browne-Ferringo, and Wang (2017) Fullan (2018)	• The role of AP remains inadequately researched. • More focus on professional knowledge and practical experience is needed. • Standards-based formation programs will help. • *More needs to be done to develop this important group of leaders.*
2020s Cusack and Bustamante (2023)	• *More can be done to develop this important group of leaders,* starting with the practices outlined in this book!

ROOTED REFLECTION

How might the APs you work with respond to the research presented above? Are they "stuck" in a certain decade? What aspects of the research surprise you the most?

ALWAYS STUCK IN SECOND GEAR

We face a critical demand for high quality school leaders, yet many of the preparation programs range in quality from inadequate to poor (Levine, 2005). As the two of us studied the challenges, and conducted research, we landed on the same conclusion: the entire field of leadership theory, mindset, and research has been woefully stalled in a morass of well-meaning intentions rather than a well-executed implementation. Like The Rembrandts sang in the theme song of the TV show *Friends*, it's like we "are always stuck in second gear."

> The entire field of leadership theory, mindset, and research has been woefully stalled in well-meaning intentions rather well-executed implementation.

The research of the last five decades makes it clear that sound approaches to leadership development may flourish *on paper*—in academic papers, professional books, and in file drawers—but actual follow-through has largely failed. No one has managed to define and popularize a set of consistent, strategic learning experiences. In *Great Teaching by Design*, John Hattie and his coauthors (2020) suggest that the solution lies in doing a better job of connecting our potential to implementation. These authors explore the relationships between potential and implementation in the graphic in Figure 1.3. Figure 1.3 helps us think about what it takes to design effective training that takes talent from intention to implementation and beyond—to mastery leadership. In short, what happens along the journey.

The way we see it, assistant and vice principal training and development is stuck at "intention." It is for this reason that we provide you with the contextual and academic information you need to move your localized leadership development farther than ever before. As a first step, let's conceptualize the process with a new working metaphor. We invite you to journey with us as we explore four big roots of leadership development that will help you realize greater leadership capacity in your aspiring school leaders.

FIGURE 1.3   MOVING FROM POTENTIAL TO IMPLEMENTATION

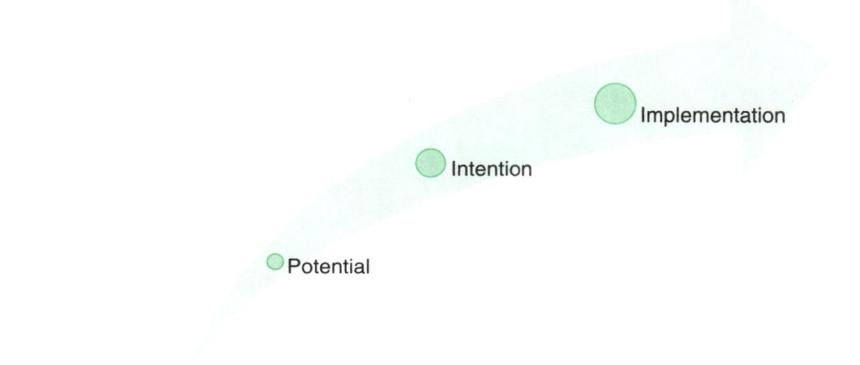

Source: Hattie, Bustamante, Almarode, Fisher, & Frey (2020).

A NEW METAPHOR FOR GROWTH AND DEVELOPMENT

Source: iStock.com/Venezia7

Education is full of rich and colorful metaphors which often are used to describe a context or situation. For example, the need to have a steady supply of people to take on the role of school leaders is often described as a "pipeline." Some school leadership scholars propose that we create a principal pipeline so there is a steady supply of available, trained people ready to assume the role. While we like the analogy's implication of a predictable flow, we contend that the pipeline concept is flawed, and even perpetuates the challenge of scarcity. Why? Because a pipeline implies that the same commodity at entry point is what we expect to see at its terminus. Put water, oil or gas in at point A; that's what you get at point Z.

A pipeline mentality also keeps us seeing growth as linear, which it's not. Traditionally, we begin with the classroom teacher who is promoted to teacher leader, then to AP, then to principal. We have often used the sheer march of time as the litmus test for readiness to assume positions as principals. However, the traditional pipeline isn't working so well which is why we are in this crisis.

We believe that a better metaphor is a winding tree-lined pathway because the development of APs must accommodate curves. Mentoring must have a plan for celebrating the peaks and vistas, and for coaching novices to anticipate the switchbacks and valleys. Further, pathways provide milestones to those hiking that trail, a reassuring sense that someone else has been here. Someone else has traveled this route and perhaps even left a sign of their passage. We will sketch out this analogy more in a moment, but for now, a bit about the place of dire concern from which the impetus for this book sprang.

A year ago, as we looked at earlier research and talked with aspiring leaders and veteran principals, we were shocked by the dearth of a firm, clear vision. Frameworks and protocols were few and far between, and when they existed, they were procedural. School principalship is a job that demands specific leadership attributes, and yet no one seemed to be operating with an established set of them. How can the preparation of leaders be purposeful and efficient without them? Where was a model that outlined the steps of the journey and inspired educators? We decided to develop a model ourselves.

As Vince and I developed our model, we kept thinking about how steadfast leaders need to be and knew that roots were an important part of our thinking. On walks, we often see that a tree's roots are exposed at the surface, helping us appreciate how wide and deep they go, as they tap into the rich soil and water table to sustain the tree. As human beings, we often talk about our family roots; the customs, traditions, and people that ground us in who we are and keep us connected to what we value. In a leadership model, the roots, we knew, would give aspiring leaders steady, clear mentoring. We wrote down a first draft of the principles that grounded our thinking:

- *Leadership is not a linear progression*
- *Time cannot be the only determining factor for leadership effectiveness*
- *Across districts, there needs to be a higher degree of agreement regarding the attributes of effective leadership*

- *Practical experiences for aspiring leaders must be relevant and impactful*

- *Aspiring principals and leaders need clear, consistent communication at every step of the journey*

In reviewing our list, we saw that what each idea had in common was communication and relationship-building. Developing leaders must be centered on equipping all involved with the rules of engagement—from building trust to sticking to transparent standards. To us, the answer lay in harnessing the power of human motivation and knowing what supports people in becoming who they want to be. So, drawing upon the work of Albert Bandura and other seminal research, our model centers on self-efficacy and how social cognitive learning theory can help create conditions for better leadership preparation. Taken together, we affectionately call our model *The Roots of School Leader Preparation* (Figure 1.4).

FIGURE 1.4   THE ROOTS OF SCHOOL LEADER PREPARATION

Effective School Leadership

Our tree is only as strong as its roots

Leadership Standards

Culture for Implementation

Guided Leadership Experiences

Attaining Mastery Experiences

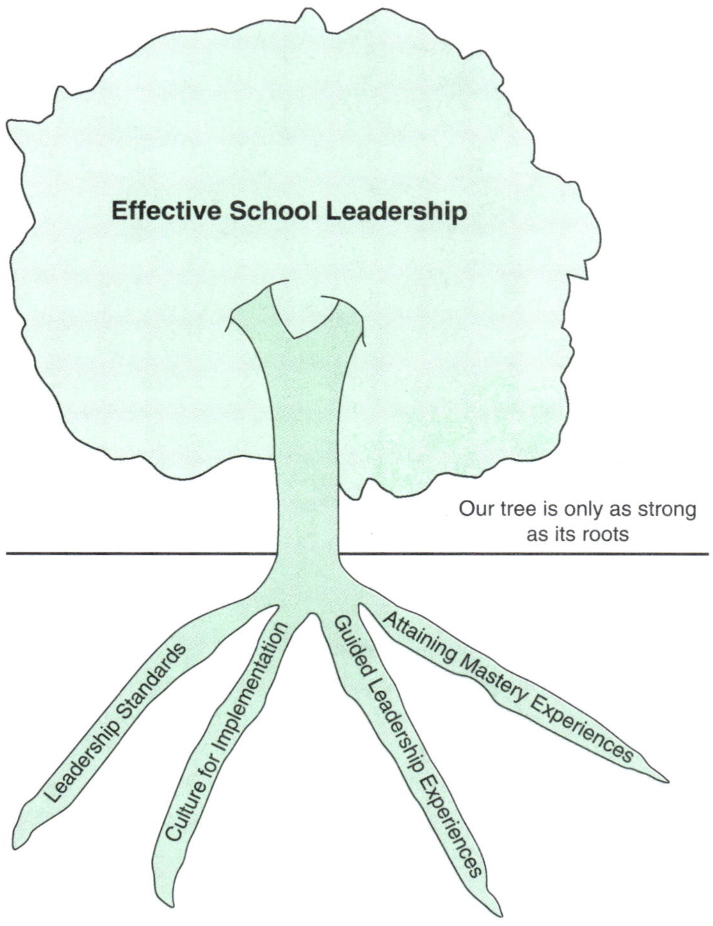

FOUR ROOTS OF SCHOOL LEADER PREPARATION

Accounting for much of the leadership research and the research on implementation we think there are four essential roots that strengthen the preparation of our future leaders. They are:

1. Raising the Bar on Leadership Standards
2. Creating a Culture for Implementation
3. Planning Guided Leadership Experiences
4. Attaining Mastery Experiences

FOUR ROOTS OF SCHOOL LEADER PREPARATION

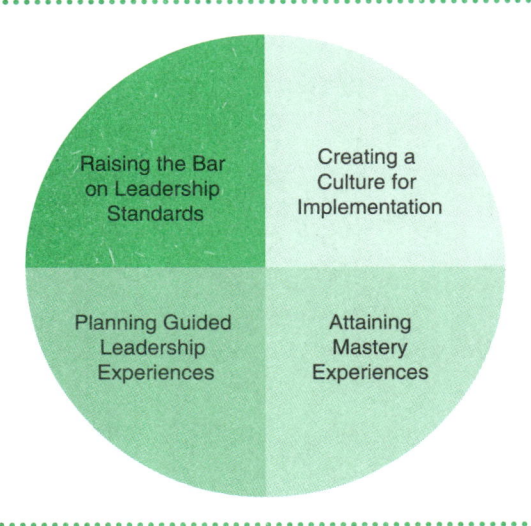

For now, let's look at the main characteristics of each root.

#1 Raising the Bar on Leadership Standards

Leadership standards may be the "mother" of all roots. The standards we propose stemmed from examining various sets of leadership standards from around the globe; later we'll guide you on how to feel confident in tweaking the standards to reflect your particular setting. The important thing is that you consistently and wholly use the standards as they are the root from which all APs' foundational knowledge develops. The assumption of principalship requires individuals to gain a corpus of knowledge and skills that often moves them beyond the mandate of their role as an AP. Leadership quality standards are therefore meant to establish a *systematic, rigorous, and practical* approach to increasing principal readiness and efficacy in addition to providing a metric that might be used to assess a principal's overall performance (Australian Institute for Teaching and School Leadership, 2014). We will explore how leveraging your state or jurisdictional standards can provide a common language and foundation upon which to predicate your formation programming.

#2 Creating a Culture for Implementation

While the leadership standards are all about consistency and universality, this next component is in a sense the opposite. To create the right conditions for an aspiring leader, we want to particularize the environment based on them as individuals. We need to begin by asking them questions, learning about them. Their interests, their

> *This model of training for our aspiring school leaders balances education, experiential learning, and mastery of skills which all revolve around a set of leadership standards.*

perceived strengths, and areas in need of development. Their curiosities. When we determine what dispositions and strengths the aspiring leaders bring with them, we can better understand how they can complement existing leadership at your site. This will lead to what is considered an "optimum learning environment," that has a certain "feel," a culture conducive to risk-taking, candor, and trust.

An environment conducive to growing leaders rests on the thinking and research on collective efficacy (DeWitt, 2021) and collegial trust (Tschannen-Moran & Gareis, 2015). Collective efficacy practices help to harmonize the learning culture through the development of instructional, managerial, and relational leadership strategies. The five facets of collegial trust—vulnerability, benevolence, honesty, openness, and competence—build the backbone of effective mentorship. By meeting our aspiring leaders where they are at and understanding which specific domains of professional learning require growth, we can best design environments that foster impactful leadership development.

#3 Planning Guided Leadership Experiences

Mentorship and coaching are key to the development of aspiring school leaders. Many school authorities offer a range of support intended for the mentoring of new school leaders, including professional learning consortia, professional associations and organizations yet, only a few focus solely on the development of APs. In many cases, the only support in place is the principal. We know that given the increased demands on principals, there is often little time and attention given to how to effectively mentor their AP(s). Influenced by Social Cognitive Learning Theory, we will explore how through the creation of vicarious leadership experiences, jurisdictions can better equip their principals in supporting the mentoring of APs.

#4 Attaining Mastery Experiences

Through the establishment of high impact experiential-based learning opportunities, aspiring principals will have greater exposure to unique leadership opportunities that are generally reserved for principals themselves. Whether modeled for them, or whether they have had time to participate in them alongside leaders, the next step is for current principals to provide space for them to take the lead by designing mastery experiences. In this case our aspiring leaders can have real-world leadership experiences with little risk of failure. The mentor's role is to continue to support with feedback, but also recognize when a high level of proficiency has occurred—and possibly even mastery.

This in part means moving from observation to integration, like including aspiring school leaders in the process of site-based decision-making. The level of integration and challenge will be constructed and navigated depending on the perceived level of proficiency and confidence that our aspiring leader has. Existing leaders or mentors must also continue to provide illustrative language for proficiency so that it can be celebrated when attained. This type of acknowledgment fuels the confidence and grit needed for success when the role of principal officially begins for aspiring leaders.

It is through this framework that we believe we can establish a stronger, more comprehensive root system that is sure to nurture and grow capable, efficacious school leaders. These roots represent the content for the next few chapters. To ensure you gain the most out of each root, we have provided a predictive inquiry activity (to be completed after this section). It is our hope you will glean information to support your leadership development as it fits your context best. Here is an overview of the key elements for Chapters 2 to 5:

Chapter Takeaways

Chapter 2: Raising the Bar on Leadership Standards

- Standards set direction for development programs
- Standards provide a metric
- Standards provide trainees with competencies to develop
- Standards inform daily practice

Chapter 3: Creating a Culture for Implementation

- Discover the feel of the environment
- Engage in active listening
- Determine the skill, will and thrill of your people
- Discern affective state

- Leverage social persuasion

- Tailor feedback

Chapter 4: Planning Guided Leadership Experiences

- Level 1 Experiences: Observation

- Level 2 Experiences: Partnered/guided practice

- Level 3 Experiences: Full responsibility

Chapter 5: Attaining Mastery Experiences

- Providing mastery experiences (increasing skill, will, and thrill)

- Giving and receiving feedback

- Knowing when mastery is achieved (expert noticing)

- Celebrating the mastery experiences (realizing greater capacity)

Before moving to the next chapter, take a few minutes to engage in a predictive inquiry-focused activity. Jot down your prediction of what each chapter will address. Also write down questions you may have right now regarding each of the roots. As you plan meetings with your principals or other colleagues, we encourage you to use the form as an opening activity. You can come back to your predictions and questions throughout the training process.

PREDICTIVE INQUIRY

Roots of School Leader Preparation

ROOT #1: RAISING THE BAR ON LEADERSHIP STANDARDS	
I predict this chapter will address:	Questions I have about Root #1:

ROOT #2: CREATING A CULTURE FOR IMPLEMENTATION	
I predict this chapter will address:	Questions I have about Root #2:

ROOT #3: PLANNING GUIDED LEADERSHIP EXPERIENCES	
I predict this chapter will address:	Questions I have about Root #3:

ROOT #4: ATTAINING MASTERY EXPERIENCES	
I predict this chapter will address:	Questions I have about Root #4:

CHAPTER 2

....

RAISING THE BAR ON LEADERSHIP STANDARDS

We make no apologies for setting high standards.
–Nancy L. Zimpher

In the previous chapter, we likened the development of leaders to the growth of a tree with a strong root system from which our strength and capability grows. We will now spend some time examining the first root, Leadership Standards.

First, a quick exercise: What comes to mind with the word "standard?" Perhaps you think of a manual transmission sports car, and the sheer mechanics of the gears. Maybe you think of "standard" as something that is basic and mass-produced, like a military uniform, standard issue. Sometimes "standard" carries associations of personal favorites, as in ice cream flavors and pizza toppings. Buildings must be "up to code" which is a specified standard of quality. Eggs, meat, and other commodities are "graded" to reflect a particular standard of quality. Standards help us discern what qualities are desirable versus those which are not. In a work setting, the word conjures expectations of quality. We use the established criteria to measure performance. All these possible meanings are how leadership standards can operate. But first they must exist, and we have to learn to make them fully operationalized.

As we asserted in the previous chapter, it is one thing to intend to apply something effectively, and it's another to implement it well. This is true with leadership standards, for sure. Following are three voices from the field (aliases provided) sharing their perceptions of challenges and opportunities tied to leadership quality standards as documented by Tim (Cusack, 2020). Each

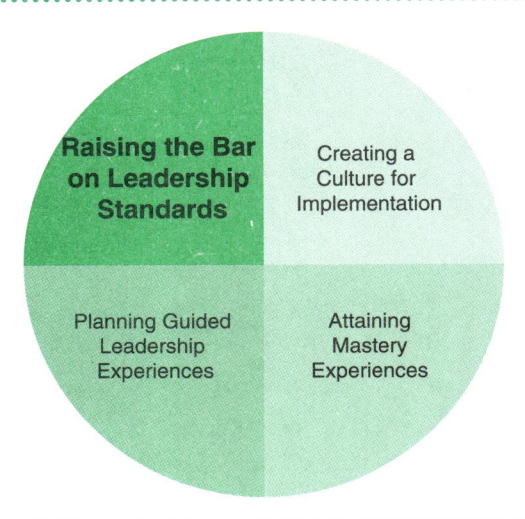

of these individuals had 10 or more years of classroom teaching experience prior to becoming an assistant principal. We would invite you to carry their words with you as you read this chapter.

LISTENING TO THE VOICES OF ASSISTANT PRINCIPALS

Coralee "The demands on a principal seem overwhelming. There are so many different things to learn! I feel ill-prepared to effectively fulfill the role at this time. Mentorship from my principal is critical to teach me the skills necessary to be a competent leader."

Juanita "I feel that to fully take on the role of principal, I need to be comfortable with the different dimensions of the Leader Quality Standard (LQS). Unfortunately, I don't get a lot of opportunities to engage with many of those responsibilities listed in the standards. This limits my ability to perform tasks as an administrator as defined by the LQS."

Pat "I aspire to be a school principal so I can continue to learn as well as lead a learning community that is inclusive and fosters all standards of the LQS and supports teachers in the Teacher Quality Standard (TQS). Ongoing mentorship and professional development with the standards, having the mindset of a lifelong learner, and being flexible will help."

Coralee, Juanita, and Pat have similar years of experience as teachers and as assistant principals, yet they differ in their desire to pursue principalship. What accounts for those differences is not a single factor, and we'll be looking at all the factors in the course of this book. But for now, what's striking is that all three of these educators are uneasy about their grasp of the skills and attributes of the leadership standards. What's also evident is that the steady role of the mentor is largely absent, especially with the first two quotes.

WHAT DO LEADERSHIP STANDARDS DO FOR US?

Leadership standards help us articulate consistency of expected performance. They also provide a way to layer accountability and assurance into a school system. We promote and demote based on these benchmarks and manage stakeholder expectations with them. It all sounds quite chilly and mechanistic, no? To some extent, that's the point—they provide universal norms. But to humanize our understanding of standards, we like to think of them as the required dispositions of effective leaders. The dispositions combine the skills, attributes, and behaviors of those who guide others in a school or a district.

> *Leadership standards help us articulate a preferred consistency of expected performance.*

The challenge, of course, is this: Who gets to decide which skills and qualities to value, and how they are measured? And what happens when standards vary from place to place, or even person to person within a school? It is for this reason that the two of us are so enthusiastic about well-articulated—and adhered to—standards, because they can have a harmonizing effect, greatly reducing variance of leadership styles within school districts.

So, the work before us is twofold: First, we need to articulate standards very well, so they work for many different people and locations. Second, we need to ensure that the standards are actually used, and that we keep various states, provinces, and countries' interpretation of them to a minimum.

To do this work, we need to look broadly. In fact, that's what our research in 2020 did—it examined the leadership standards from various jurisdictions around the world (Cusack, 2020). We sought to discover the *similarities* across the globe, as a way to root leadership standards in a set of competencies that are as universally valued as possible. These competencies "roll up" into the "universal standards" discussed in this chapter.

The similarities between standards give us all a throughline, making it easier for us to link all assistant principal development across a district to established standards. When the two of us worked together in our division's

Learning Services Department, having this bird's-eye view of many countries' standards helped us in our professional development work as we named teacher and leader competencies. This isn't to say that developing learning around them is easy work. Unpacking standards and providing clear examples of them for others alone is hard, to say nothing of guiding aspiring leaders to embody them over several years. But what we discovered is that the standards provide a common language, and that fact alone is hugely beneficial. Why? Because all of this work rests on effective communication.

In addition, having a common language of desired competencies (what school leaders must be able to know, understand, and do) is critical to fostering a leader's self-efficacy. Realizing higher levels of self-efficacy in assistant principals (and teachers for that matter) is essential to understanding how to attract more aspiring leaders to principalship.

What Research Tells Us About Standards

Around 2015, many educational jurisdictions and authorities placed increased focus on articulating the necessary competencies and skills that school leaders must espouse (Liu, Xu, Grant, Strong, & Fang, 2015). Research by the Wallace Foundation (2015) and the Council of Chief State School Officers (CCSSO, 2015) indicated that there was no nation-wide consistency in processes surrounding principal supervision. The prevailing thinking in the ongoing professional conversation was that standards helped to address a knowledge gap pertinent to the supervision of school leaders (Wallace Foundation, 2015). It also became evident that established standards weren't the only thing in need of development: effective preparation models were needed too, as the following citations express:

- High-quality school leadership preparatory programs must be sourced in relevant and rigorous standards (Lehman, Boyland, & Sriver, 2014).

- The implementation of leadership quality standards requires a carefully considered delivery model (Leithwood & Mascall, 2008).

- Regardless of who is supervising the implementation of standards, there are often deficiencies of the right development and support to help school leaders, particularly novice principals and assistant principals, to build capacity in the domain of instructional leadership (CCSSO, 2015).

The Benefits of Standards as the Basis for Training

Standards are the starting point of excellent leadership development. They provide a true north for any professional development work you are doing—and you're not alone in recognizing the need for them to reflect contemporary school cultures and needs. Over the course of the 2010s, countries such as Australia, Canada (Alberta), China, England, and the United States modernized their school leadership standards. This renaissance of standard-setting occurring over the past 25 years underscores that quality practice standards are integral to the function of leadership (Murphy, 2017). Standards benefit educators in the following four ways.

1. **Standards set direction for development programs.** Standards help us to clarify the role of aspiring principals and principals. We can literally cut and paste the standards into a digital document and have a blueprint upon which to design powerful, research-based professional learning. "Standards can be a guiding force to states and leadership preparation programs as they identify and develop the specific knowledge, skills, dispositions, and other characteristics required of educational leaders to achieve real student success in school" (CCSSO, 2015, p. 5). In our context (Alberta) we call these specific attributes a *competency*. Similar to the Council of Chief State School Officers's (CCSSO) wording, we define competency as an interrelated set of knowledge, skills, and attitudes developed over time.

2. **Standards provide a metric.** With a clear set of competencies required for the job, leaders can then use these as a way to assess a (school leader's) overall performance (ATA, 2019; Australian Institute for Teaching and School Leadership [AITSL], 2014; Dinham, Collarbone, Evans, & Mackay, 2013). Knowing the performance criteria to which they are being held accountable is paramount for assistant principals (anyone for that matter). We want to make it clear though that a set of competencies is not the only criteria to consider for robust formative and summative evaluation. In order to determine what support may be needed to support assistant principals in becoming conversant with leadership standards, it is important to understand what specific areas assistant principals might identify as requiring further professional development. There are other performatory elements to consider (which we will explore in Chapter 4: Providing Guided-Learning Experiences).

   > *We define competency as an interrelated set of knowledge, skills and attitudes developed over time.*

3. **Standards provide trainees with competencies to develop.** Human development and education are a two-way street. That is, the

competencies inform program design and the way talent is assessed—*and* the competencies can be used by the aspiring leaders! They inform, they inspire, and they serve as lights along each person's unique professional journey. As we will explore in later chapters, mentors and mentees use these competencies to develop individual growth plans.

4. **Standards inform daily practice**. Professional standards need to be firmly in place in order for principals to understand and be able to improve teaching and learning. Additionally, standards centered upon research competencies known to enhance teaching and learning are essential to transforming schools in the context of continuous improvement. Leadership standards, therefore, offer the opportunity to look at job roles and function systematically across multidimensional domains and present indicators designed to articulate the skills needed for role success. We will guide you to look at your local standards with these four benefits in mind, but first we want you to be informed by what educators in other parts of the world have done.

ROOTED REFLECTION

What is the value of leadership standards? Does your state or jurisdiction have an established slate of standards? To what extent are you using them?

STANDARDS AROUND THE WORLD

A fulsome exploration and analysis of jurisdictions that make great use of common standards is beyond the scope of this book, but we will provide an overview of several countries and regions that have recently updated their practice standards. As part of our overview, we will seek to understand what aspects of leadership are universal to school leadership formation and appreciate the mix of interpersonal and ethical facets with more explicit, quantifiable characteristics. We will examine the following: Alberta, Australia, the United Kingdom, Abu Dhabi, and the United States (see Figure 2.1). We have selected these five examples as they tend to be the foundation for many other countries and jurisdictions around the world. We will be unpacking these over the next few pages.

Common Themes

Now that we have given an overview of the leadership standards we analyzed, we would like to recommend a thinking activity (Activity 2.1). Have a look at the five sets of standards in Figure 2.1 and tease out the common themes. We have left space for you to write this directly in the book. Please complete Activity 2.1 before looking at Figure 2.2 where we note our own observations of common themes.

FIGURE 2.1 LEADERSHIP STANDARDS FROM AROUND THE GLOBE

UNITED STATES: PROFESSIONAL STANDARDS FOR EDUCATIONAL LEADERS (PSEL), FORMALLY ILLSC	ALBERTA, CANADA: LEADERSHIP QUALITY STANDARD (LQS)
1. Mission, vision, and core values 2. Ethics and professional norms 3. Equity and cultural responsiveness 4. Curriculum, instruction and assessment 5. Community of care and support for students 6. Professional capacity of school personnel 7. Professional community for teachers and staff 8. Meaningful engagement of families and community 9. Operations and management 10. School improvement	1. Fostering effective relationships 2. Modeling commitment to professional learning 3. Embodying visionary leadership 4. Leading a learning community 5. Foundational knowledge first nations, metis, and inuit 6. Providing instructional leadership 7. Building leadership capacity 8. Managing school operations 9. Larger societal context 10. Catholic leadership (separate boards)
AUSTRALIA: THE STANDARD (AUS)	**ABU DHABI: ABU DHABI EDUCATION COUNCIL TEACHER AND EDUCATIONAL LEADERSHIP STANDARDS (ADEC)**
1. Leading teaching and learning 2. Developing self and others 3. Leading improvement, innovation, and change 4. Leading the management of the school 5. Engaging and working with the community	1. Leading strategically 2. Leading teaching and learning 3. Leading the organization 4. Leading people 5. Leading the community

UNITED KINGDOM: HEADTEACHERS' STANDARDS (UK)
1. School culture (builds on Teachers' Standards 1) 2. Teaching (builds on Teachers' Standards 2 and 4) 3. Curriculum and assessment (builds on Teachers' Standards 3 and 6) 4. Behavior (builds on Teachers' Standards 7) 5. Additional and special educational needs (builds on Teachers' Standards 5) 6. Professional development (some match to Teachers' Standards 4) 7. Organizational management 8. School improvement 9. Working in partnership 10. Governance and accountability

Source: National Policy Board for Educational Administration (2015), Alberta Education (2018), Australian Institute for Teaching and School Leadership (2014), Abu Dhabi Education Council (2018), Crown (2020).

ACTIVITY 2.1: DISCERNING THE COMMON THEMES IN EDUCATIONAL LEADERSHIP STANDARDS

COMMON THEMES	STANDARDS

FIGURE 2.2   COMMON THEMES ACROSS THE EDUCATIONAL LEADERSHIP STANDARDS

COMMON THEMES	STANDARDS
We noticed that assistant principals must engage in supporting *great teaching and learning.* Theme = Learning and Engagement	PSEL #4 & 7; LQS #3, 4 & 6; AUS #1, 2 & 5; ADEC #2; and UK #2, 3, 4, 5 & 6.
We observed that assistant principals must leverage a variety of *resources* in serving the *operational* needs of the school. Theme = Resources and Operations	PSEL #9; LQS #8; AUS #4 & 5; ADEC #3 & 4; and UK #7.
We noted that assistant principals must understand the school *culture* in support of the wider *community.* Theme = Community and Culture	PSEL #1, 3, 5, & 8; LQS #8; AUS #4 & 5; ADEC #5; and UK #1 & 9.
We found that assistant principals must be *innovative* in seeking ways to support school growth and *improvement.* Theme = Growth and Innovation	PSEL #10; LQS #3 & 7; AUS #3; ADEC #1 & 3; and UK #8 & 10.

Here's what we noticed: While we can readily classify the various standards in many ways such as instructional, managerial, and moral (ethical) domains, we noticed four general categories that are common to all five sets of standards. We would argue that these are universal and might be considered the norm (or normative) for a basis of leadership standards. Figure 2.2 lists what we observed to be common to the five sets of leadership standards featured in Figure 2.1.

Notice that several common themes appear across the standards. For example, *engagement* can mean getting learners (students and staff) excited about what they are learning, and it also could mean how we connect with our community or a group of stakeholders, e.g., parents and guardians to solicit feedback. In the daily work of schools and leadership development, these themes are referred to as *competencies*. Importantly, though, we want to emphasize that competencies aren't merely skills. They are more than that. Competencies are an interrelated set of knowledge, skills, and attitudes developed over time and drawn upon and applied to a particular leadership context in order to support quality leadership, teaching, and optimum learning (Alberta Education, LQS, 2019). In other words, the themes we identified can permeate through multiple categories. When we looked at standards from across the globe, we noticed they fit best in the following four general categories:

1. Learning and Engagement

2. Resources and Operations

3. Community and Culture

4. Growth and Innovation

We call these the universal leadership standards.

USING UNIVERSAL LEADERSHIP STANDARDS TO INFORM TRAINING

In Appendix 3, we unpack the standards of these five locations, providing commentary for each one. We encourage you to read it and share it with colleagues as part of your professional development work. That said, in our quest to focus your efforts on implementation, the overview above is sufficient to move forward. We invite you to our research-based "shortcut," the universal leadership standards. Use them as your blueprint. Following them are a number of steps we recommend to launch and sustain leadership standards-based development.

Our universal standards of leadership are inspired and informed by international leadership standards, so they draw from the research and work of many educators around the world. If you are reading this book and aren't familiar with your local leadership standards, or work in an area that doesn't have an established list of standards, you can count on the universal

FIGURE 2.3   THE UNIVERSAL LEADERSHIP STANDARDS

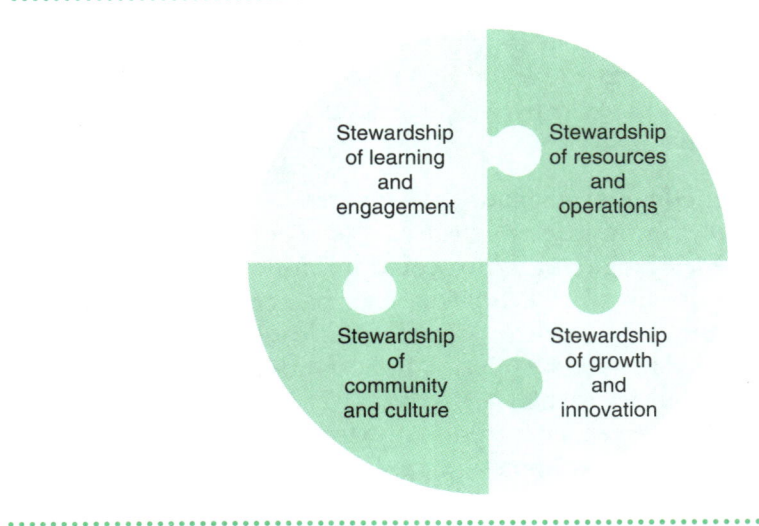

standards. If you are reading this with a group of leaders from other different jurisdictions (like in a book study model), these standards can be used as discussion points for conversation.

A Stewardship Approach to Leading

Following Figure 2.3 is a summary of our "universal leadership standards." Notice that our use of the term "Stewardship" is purposeful, conveying our conviction that every effective leader operates with a deep sense of responsibility to care for others.

Stewardship of Learning and Engagement: This leadership standard reflects all capacities of instructional leadership. This may include decisions that directly impact the students, staff, and community stakeholders. Leaders who implement this standard acknowledge the impact of high-quality instruction on student learning and achievement.

Stewardship of Resources and Operations: This leadership standard reflects all capacities of managerial and adherence to state regulations or legislation. This may include decisions involving the deployment of finances, human capital, materials, and infrastructure to best support the learning community.

Stewardship of Community and Culture: This leadership standard reflects all capacities of moral and ethical leadership. This may include the fostering of collegial and communal trust, and inclusive and caring communities. Leaders who focus on this standard consciously create supportive environments to best serve all students in their community.

Stewardship of Growth and Innovation: This leadership standard reflects all capacities of continuous growth and systems excellence. This includes promoting opportunities for ongoing growth for all stakeholders. Leaders who focus on this standard create conditions for innovation and creativity through an environment that embraces risk-taking and experiential learning.

Please note, these standards are meant to be used as guideposts for conversations with colleagues and may not completely reflect the unique realities of your leadership or jurisdictional context.

LISTENING TO THE VOICES OF SALVADOR GUTIERREZ AND LILIANA CRAIGHT

Assistant Principal Salvador Gutierrez and Principal Liliana Craight have served Memorial Middle School as the leadership team for 5 years. In those 5 years, they have encountered almost all there is to experience when you look at the general portfolio of school leadership. They are considered one of the more efficient leadership teams in their school district. One of the reasons for this is their fidelity to the district leadership standards. Their district has the same leadership standards for Principals as well as Assistant Principals, which leads to a common understanding of the expectations of leadership.

At the beginning of every school year Salvador and Liliana sit down to look at the leadership standards and plan their focus for the year. This practice started becoming regular as Ms. Craight noticed a considerable difference of interpretation of the standards depending on the leadership position. This year their leadership focus will be on Managerial and Operational improvements (see universal standard 2). Liliana begins the meeting with the following discussion question: *how might you interpret your roles and responsibilities when it comes to meeting this standard of leadership?* Both Salvador and Liliana take 10 minutes to individually write down their perspectives, and upon reflection they engage in the conversation around this question.

"I see my role here as the leader who supports the daily functions and operations of the school with scheduling, supporting teachers' requests for building assistance and coordinating supervision for lunch time," Salvador begins. "Ah, very interesting," Liliana replied, "I see my role as principal as the leader who coordinates support from our district to ensure the school operates on the macro level. Things like budget, employee hiring, and resource allocation."

Conversations like this are eye opening for both the principal and assistant principal because in this case Liliana ensures that as the school year unfolds that Salvador is involved in principal level operations discussions. Similarly, she ensures that she takes on some of the responsibilities that Salvador outlined to make sure there is a collaborative leadership approach. When asked about why she felt this was important, her answer was as follows. "Salvador is a brilliant assistant principal, and it is my hope that when he becomes a principal in the very near future, he will have had exposure to many of the decisions I make as principal. Also, it is important for me as a leader to understand the context of my assistant principal in order to support them as best as I can. This also gives me the opportunity to trade responsibilities with him to ensure there is an equal understanding that we are both leaders in our school."

Perspective is everything. As we see in the case of Liliana and Salvador, depending on which context of leadership you approach, there will be a different interpretation of your roles and responsibilities in relation to the standard. That is why it is fundamentally important to engage in conversations across leadership roles to ensure all perspectives are acknowledged.

Following are a few examples of actions you can take to integrate the standards into the fabric of your leadership development. These suggestions are crafted to indicate the approximate time it may take to engage in these actions, as well as examples of what they may look like in practice. Remember these actions should not be undertaken in isolation, but rather can be combined to develop your leadership capacities.

Meet to Discuss the Standards: Monthly Conversations

Description: The first step for you is to plan *when* you and colleagues will gather to unpack and understand standards in your current assistant principal development programs. We have found it works best to schedule a larger chunk of time to meet before the school year begins, and then revisit this at intervals of every four to six weeks throughout the school year.

Examples: Within our jurisdiction we invite every assistant principal to complete a survey whereby they identify the three leadership competencies they want to go deeper with. These data are shared with central system leadership. This helps various departments to craft experiences and opportunities that explicitly address the chosen competencies. We are able to see trends where we may want to add a more global (divisional) focus and we also can determine where some smaller learning group or targeted individual support (professional learning) may be leveraged. Assistant principals work with their identified areas on an ongoing basis with not only their principal, but also with leadership support team members from our central office. In 2021, we shifted from a Fall planning timeframe to late

Spring. Knowing what one's focus is in late May for the upcoming school year has been well received by our assistant principals as it allows for key summer reading and advance planning so that being September-ready is less stressful.

Focus on a Few Standards at a Time

Description: Developing the complete understanding of our leadership standards requires us to foster growth "an inch wide and a mile deep." When our assistant principals select only a few of the standards to develop they can better track their progress to mastery without the feeling of being too overwhelmed. Choosing two to three standards and then deeply engaging in practice will result in a greater capacity for leadership development. This requires frequent conversations to determine when the aspiring leader is ready to shift focus.

Example: As mentioned earlier, we ask our assistant principals to select no more than three goals. We want to ensure there is ample time allocated to go deep in each area. In Alberta, the Alberta Teachers' Association (ATA) provides a great online tool that allows users to see the pallet of quality standards that exist and helps streamline areas for focus. This has been particularly effective in honing the plan while minimizing the amount of time required to write it.

Standards as Success Criteria for Leadership Meetings (i.e., Every Meeting)

Description: Success criteria are better known as statements that drive the learning and development of classrooms. Yet, we've found that including these statements as part of leadership meetings brings great clarity and focus to the meeting. Even better is when we use the standards as the statements for success/expectations. This maintains the significance of the leadership standards, as well as encourages fluency of understanding for leaders and aspiring leaders alike.

Example: Within our jurisdiction, our curricular consultants, operations support team, and central leadership support staff make explicit links to the leadership standards. For example, if attending a session on budgeting school resources, the assistant principals will observe from the facilitator which elements of the school resources and operations management indicators they are addressing in that session. We have this strategy hardwired into all of our professional learning (including teachers). Just as we know what letter Sesame Street was brought to us by…we ensure our aspiring leaders know the intentional link (relevance) to the leader quality standard we are exploring at that moment. This has been well received!

Director of IT and Innovation at The International School of Curitiba (ISC)—Brazil

The International School of Curitiba is a nondenominational, private international school. It consists of slightly over 700 students from early childhood education through to high school. In November 2020, I was called upon by our board of directors to take over as Interim Head of School (HOS) as our current HOS was suddenly removed from his duties. When the leader of any institution is suddenly removed, you have a major breach of trust. To further complicate the matter, we were in the midst of the pandemic, online, and Brazil was one of the worst countries in the world for COVID-19 (we would eventually become #1 for daily new cases during my tenure). As I took over as the Head of School, I knew I would have to put a great deal of time and effort into rebuilding trust. I had to think deeply about stewardship of community and culture. I was lucky in that the school community knew me already and I had many positive relationships established. However, they had never seen me in this capacity before. I immediately opened the lines of communication in a variety of ways in order to keep parents engaged, informed, and to build capacity even further. My multipronged approach involved weekly webinars featuring leadership, teachers or students on a variety of topics, reaching out to parent groups to set up Zoom meetings, regular email announcements, and making myself available for communication consistently. Likewise, this rebuilding of trust also had to be focused inwardly as well. Weekly webinars were held with our teachers and operational staff, with a focus on celebrating the excellent teaching and learning taking place at the school. It was also vital that a culture of high expectations was maintained with our staff. This has always been a part of ISC culture, whether on the teaching side or the operational side, and maintaining this was important to keep morale high and the focus on students.

While doing the essential work of supporting teaching and learning, it is important not to neglect thinking about and developing skill sets toward the stewardship of operations and resources. As a rising leader, it is just as important to verse yourself in this area of leadership. As Interim HOS I was very quickly tasked with making key decisions in this area. As mentioned earlier, our HOS has been removed, and at that time, we were also without a Director of Finance and Operations. I was thrust into a temporary position of managing school finances and our operational budget. This involved key decisions around classroom resources, school repairs, professional learning, and general operational expenses. Having a background in business certainly helped. As a leader it is imperative that you upskill yourself in financial management in order to understand and participate in this side of the school. Furthermore, I was also intricately involved in hiring, both for teaching positions and operational staff. Understanding how to conduct interviews, what to look for in candidates, and the needs of the school in terms of potential hires were all critical to finding the right fit for ISC. As an aspiring leader you may have not had much exposure to infrastructure projects in a school setting but being versed in school repair processes and new infrastructure can be helpful. As I shifted into the HOS role, there were several campus projects that instantly became mine to oversee and manage. These included outdoor learning spaces as we prepared to open our campus, a second drop-off area to spread students out, and general repairs. I had to quickly develop skills around contracts, timelines, worker safety, campus down time, and a host of other considerations. I would highly encourage any aspiring leader to seek out opportunities to learn about this area as it will only serve to help you in your leadership journey.

Mastery of Standards

The appreciation, understanding, and application of leadership standards are paramount to the success of aspiring school leaders. By encouraging conversations and creating more practical opportunities to apply standards in realistic settings, we can increase leadership capacity and generate experiences that lead to mastery. Mastery experience addresses the need for school leaders to have a level of competency with the essential knowledge and skills commensurate to those articulated in leadership standards (CCSSO, 2015). This concept of mastery of standards is commonplace in the role of principal but has sadly been lacking in other leadership capacities in schools, especially assistant principals.

When you synthesize the research and common concerns by leading institutions regarding the model for developing assistant principals and sustaining their leadership in the schools, one thing is apparent. There is a need for a development model for aspiring principals that is focused on the knowledge, attitudes, and actions of principals when delivered through the lens of leadership standards. This is where we go next. Using the *universal leadership standards* we proposed earlier in this chapter, we will examine the facets of leadership development that will properly prepare aspiring school leaders to take on the role of principal.

 **SYSTEM CHECK**

In seeking to better understand the importance of leadership standards as a root essential to supporting stronger leadership development, consider the following questions:

1. To what extent does your school jurisdiction use a common set of leadership standards? If you do not have a set of standards, why not?

2. How much intentional time is dedicated to unpacking and understanding standards in your current assistant principal development programs?

3. Regarding professional learning and growth plans, to what degree do your assistant principals have the opportunity to determine which leadership standard(s) they want to have greater focus?

(Continued)

(Continued)

4. Of your existing set of standards, what are the competencies where you see greatest need for improvement? Would your current principals and assistant principals agree with your observations?

5. To what extent does the concept of stewardship resonate with your vision for school leadership preparation programming?

IMPLEMENTATION POINTS TO PONDER

1. Consider surveying your school leadership teams to gauge which aspects of your existing standards are at the forefront of their perceived need as areas requiring more focus or attention.

2. Consider establishing Communities of Practice or Professional Learning Communities whereby assistant principals can connect with others with similar areas of leadership standard inquiry.

3. Consider including all members of your central leadership team in understanding which specific areas of inquiry are prevalent so that they can have greater intentionality in interactions (development sessions) with assistant principals.

PREDICTIVE INQUIRY

Use this table to compare your predictions at the end of Chapter 1 with the content presented in this chapter.

RAISING THE BAR ON LEADERSHIP STANDARDS	
Predictions that were correct:	Questions I still have:
New information learned:	

CHAPTER 3

....

CREATING A CULTURE FOR IMPLEMENTATION

Maybe you are searching among the branches for what only appears in the roots.

—Rumi

FOUR ROOTS OF SCHOOL LEADER PREPARATION

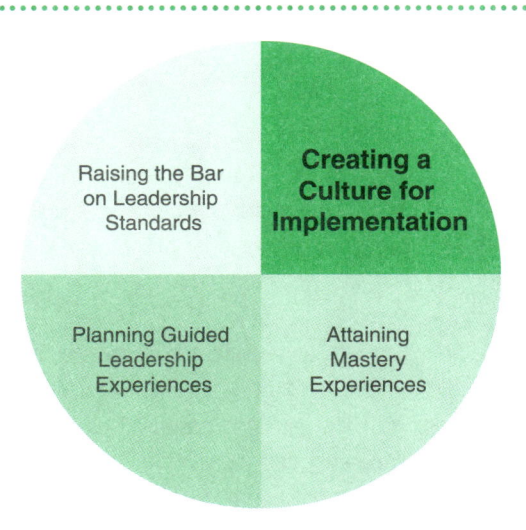

Strong roots provide the sustenance needed for growth. They draw moisture and nutrients from the soil and transport it to the leaves, and store energy for future growth. The richer the soil, the stronger the root system becomes. We are working this tree analogy more because it provides so many parallels to the development of school leaders. A fertile learning environment yields optimal conditions for leadership to take root and flourish! Let's take a look now at the second root of our leadership tree: Environment for Implementation. With this one, we explore ways in which systems leaders sustain the practical routines, collaborations, troubleshooting, and cheerleading that make implementation possible.

UNIVERSAL LEADERSHIP STANDARDS FOCUS

Community and Culture: This leadership standard reflects all capacities of moral and ethical leadership. This may include the fostering of collegial and communal trust, inclusive and caring communities. Leaders who focus on this standard consciously create supportive environments to best serve all students in their community.

LISTENING TO THE VOICES OF ASSISTANT PRINCIPALS

What do assistant principals have to say? The three quotes that follow shed light on some of the challenges and complexities of their roles. We invite you to carry these voices forward as you read this chapter, as their reflections speak to the presence of—or lack of—important conditions for sustaining growth.

Sammi (Junior High) "The principal's role has become very political, and expectations are not just difficult but unreasonable with the increased number of and level of entitlement of various stakeholders. A principal is ultimately responsible for too many things they cannot possibly manage."

Doug (High School) "My transition into an assistant principal position and subsequent experiences as an AP have left me feeling that the position will not adequately prepare me for a principalship. My understanding of the position was that I would gain a deeper understanding of all aspects of leadership and be given at least some responsibilities within the school to strengthen my leadership abilities. I do not feel that I had these opportunities with two different principals over 3 years."

Gemma (K–6) "I believe I have been working toward building my knowledge and skill base to lead a school. I have had the opportunity to work for excellent principals who have given me the opportunity to build my own leadership capacity. Although I know the learning curve will be steep and I won't fully understand all of the demands until I am in that role, I feel I have a solid foundation and am willing and able to take on this challenge."

ROOTED REFLECTION

What did you hear?

Have a look at the comments from the assistant principals above. What might be the reasons for Gemma's positive response versus Doug and Sammi's negative response?

WHAT IS A CULTURE FOR IMPLEMENTATION?

The environment in which we develop aspiring school leaders is just as important as the knowledge we are hoping to develop in them. We call this the environment for implementation. Think of the following example. Some people have a green thumb—they can grow anything anywhere, like Mark Watney (The Martian) who was able to grow potatoes in adverse conditions. Gardeners with this gift are sensitive to all the factors of growth, including the pH balance of soil, nutrients, moisture, light conditions, and temperature. They are experts and have an intuitive feel for the environment. You know where this line of thinking is going, right? You guessed it: to cultivate school leaders, you need to attend to many aspects of community and culture. You need both knowledge and intuition. The environment in which we develop leaders must contain certain conditions for optimal growth and development.

SIX ESSENTIAL ACTIONS FOR IMPLEMENTATION

1. Discover the feel of the environment

2. Engage in active listening

3. Determine the skill, will, and thrill of your people

4. Discern affective state

5. Leverage social persuasion

6. Tailor feedback

We will unpack these six moves over the course of this chapter.

Discover the Feel of the Environment

Anytime I (Vince) walk into a school for the first time, I immediately get a *feel* for the learning environment. In many of the elementary schools I visit, the focus on student success and future readiness is palpable. Pennants line the hallways. Sometimes there are glass cases of sports trophies in the entry area. In high schools, I often see posters of universities and famous destinations around the world, motivating and inspiring students to live up to their potential—go the distance, academically and literally. Become. Excel. See the world. At the risk of sounding like the Grinch, as I take in the warm, student-centeredness of it all, my professional self is getting a feel for what it all means for the *rest* of the school community. The teachers—what's in it for them? Are their potentials being intentionally noticed and nourished as well? Don't get us wrong, the primary focus of the school environment should be for the students; yet, it is also important to consider how the environment is contributing to the development of teachers and leaders. In this chapter, we help you learn to attune to all facets of the environment—visible, invisible, and implied—and to recognize how they either enable or disable professional growth.

> *Attune to all facets of the environment—visible, invisible, and implied—and recognize how they either enable or disable professional growth.*

A traditional way to determine the impact of our environment is through a collection of data, whether that be a staff survey, a suggestion box, or even formal interviews with the leadership team and teaching staff. These forms of data collection give us a true understanding of the sentiments behind the responses. We understand that this may be daunting (especially when considering formal interviews), but we can lessen the anxiety by posing a set of questions that begin with the aspiring leader's perceived strengths and successes. We then ask questions that do focus on the aspects of leadership that we deem need improvement. In this way, we are efficient—too much beating around the bush serves no one. In an interview setting, the conversation allows participants to have an open space to provide comments, which adds a voice and authenticity to the data.

This type of data collection is terrific for getting to know our aspiring leaders, keeping current with passions and concerns. However, it can only tell us so much about the environment. So, we advise you to step back and consider the stories behind the data collected, which we affectionately call discovering the "five senses" of the leadership environment. To gather information in this way, you are open to sensory information—visual, tonal, and tactile. You reflect on what you see, hear, say, and how it's received. And you reflect on your role in both creating the environment and gathering data. The following questions and suggested responses can help you begin to get a feel for the health of the leader-development culture (Figure 3.1).

FIGURE 3.1 DISCOVERING THE "FIVE SENSES" OF THE LEADERSHIP CULTURE

QUESTION	ASK YOURSELF, THEN CONSIDER THE SUGGESTED ACTION STEP
What types of language are we using in conversations with our aspiring leaders?	• Is what and how I share positive or negative in tone? Accentuate the positive. • Am I projecting my personal experiences too much on the learner? Ensure the learner has ample opportunity to share their feelings of how things are going.
What are we hearing our aspiring leaders saying about their leadership journey?	• Are there any glaring concerns? Address them in a timely fashion. • What can be celebrated? Find small successes and leverage them to increase confidence.
How is our physical environment conducive to leadership and leadership development?	• Do aspiring leaders have the amenities and tools needed to do the work asked of them? Do an environmental scan and ask what else might be needed or helpful.
How are we fostering a sense of community and trust in our learning community?	• Are conversations open, honest, and respectful of divergent opinions? Provide ample opportunity for others to share their voice and perspectives in a safe and caring environment. • Do aspiring leaders have the opportunity to connect to the broader community? Find opportunities that connect assistant principals to all stakeholder groups, for example, parents, system leaders, and community.
In faculty meetings, what are we seeing when we read the room in terms of colleagues' facial expression energy level?	• Do aspiring leaders appear engaged, ready to learn? Encourage them to be present in the moment, limit distractions, check in with each other, and provide ample opportunities for dialogue and sharing.

Engage in Active Listening

So, after getting the general feel, what exactly do you do next? We reflect on what we noticed, and we get honest with ourselves about instances when we know we fell short of being a leader. For example, if I discovered that I tended to talk too much in meetings, I'd talk less. If I noticed that my meetings started with me talking first, I would switch to allow an open forum setting at the beginning of meetings. If I realized that teachers and my assistant principal tended to use deficit language about students like "our

FIGURE 3.2 ACTIVE LISTENING

BEHAVIORS AND STATEMENTS THAT *PROMOTE* ACTIVE LISTENING	BEHAVIORS AND STATEMENTS THAT *UNDERMINE* ACTIVE LISTENING
• Listening with the intent to understand • Focus completely on the listening • Asking questions to seek understanding • Summarize key points of what you heard • Withholding judgment	• Using a cell phone, or being distracted while listening • Interrupting the speaker to interject your opinion or fact • Disengaging from the conversation because you do not agree • Exercising judgment

students are so far behind and I don't think they will catch up," I would look into the reasons why they are using this language and then have a conversation regarding asset-focused language when describing students and their learning. If after three weeks I noticed a consistent chorus of people saying they don't have time and indicating their frustrations, I would wake up and smell the coffee—they aren't being resistant to change, they are just honestly overworked, and I need to remove something from their plates. Part of active listening is modeling the behaviors that are expected of you as a leader. Figure 3.2 includes examples of behaviors that promote and undermine active listening.

Getting better with active listening in school improvement conversations and getting better at conversing effectively is a learned skill for everyone. In his book, *Collaborative Leadership*, Peter DeWitt reminds us, "... members of the team need to learn what it means to be a part of a functional and impactful team ... understanding how to implement improvement, facilitate faculty meetings around improvement ... does not come naturally to everyone" (DeWitt, 2022, p. 115).

We are going to circle back to other techniques for learning how to act on the data, but for now, we are going to go from the macro to the micro. We share tools and techniques for getting to know individuals. Once you know the particulars of your aspiring leaders, you can motivate them and mentor them to bring about universally constructive change in a school.

ROOTED REFLECTION

Take a few minutes and go for an informal learning walk-through in your school or district office. If you were to describe the "five senses" of your environment to a colleague, how might that sound? What changes might you need to implement to gain a higher degree of positive confident leaders-in-development?

Know the Skill, Will, and Thrill of Your People

The leadership in our schools is only as strong as the leadership team, and like many teams, each individual brings with them a unique set of knowledge, skills, and attitudes. Not unlike the dispositions our students have, our aspiring school leaders have unique capabilities that may be unnoticed if we do not get to know our people. Principals must *actively* engage in getting to know their assistant principals both professionally and personally. While we realize you cannot force a personal relationship, we believe there are always ways to bring about a collegial rapport that gives you sufficient insight about the individual.

This helps us build on the strengths and interests we learn of, and also allows us to make more well-considered decisions; we can anticipate the impact of our decisions when we know the *who* behind the person prior to engaging in the *what* of leadership.

> **We can anticipate the impact of our decisions when we know the who behind the person prior to engaging in the what of leadership.**

In our work in schools, we have discovered it's beneficial for principals to lean on a framework for these efforts of getting to know aspiring leaders in order to tailor coaching. We have had a positive response to a skill, will, and thrill framework modeled after research by Hattie and Donoghue on the skill, will, and thrill of student learning (Hattie & Donoghue, 2016). The framework helps us focus on three distinct categories as we engage in learning about our assistant principals.

Let us unpack how we might use the skill, will, and thrill of aspiring leaders as outlined in Figure 3.3 as a framework for cultivating talent. As always, we encourage you to get curious. Just as we encouraged you to get a feel for the school culture, and pursue answers to the five senses questions (Figure 3.1), now the questions are:

- What is the person's prior knowledge?
- What's their disposition?
- What are they most motivated by?

By understanding the skill, will, and thrill of or aspiring leaders, we can design the environment in which their leadership can flourish.

> **By understanding the skill, will, and thrill of our aspiring leaders, we can design the environment in which their leadership can flourish.**

Skill

One of the first aspects of learning about our leaders is to determine what knowledge and prior experiences they bring to the table. We also want to

FIGURE 3.3   THE SKILL, WILL, AND THRILL OF ASPIRING LEADERS

The skill of leadership refers to what prior knowledge the aspiring leader brings with them. This can be previous leadership experiences, knowledge of local leadership standards, and understandings of leadership. These are what our assistant principals bring with them to their leadership role.

The will of leadership refers to the aspiring leader and their disposition toward leading. The specific dispositions will determine how the leader may respond when confronted with new or challenging leadership situations.

The thrill of leadership refers to the leader's motivations. Essentially their passion toward leadership development, and their desires to pursue leadership at a higher level.

Source: Adapted from Hattie et al. (2020).

discover how they make meaning from their experiences (the skill). For example, what might be their level of understanding when it comes to local leadership standards? What leadership experiences do they bring with them—both from in a school setting and outside of a school setting? By deliberately inquiring along these lines, we can begin to determine where our aspiring school leader may require support. In essence, we may be able to predict areas of leadership that need to be developed so they can grow their skill. For example, an assistant principal may be seasoned and confident with instructional matters, and thus tend to devote time to this strength, but shy away from operational aspects of leading.

Consider the questions and responses from conversations held between principals and aspiring school leaders in Figure 3.4.

Will

Understanding the unique dispositions of our aspiring leaders will also play a determining role in how they may approach specific experiences. To put it simply, the will is what our aspiring leaders will look to when they are confronted with a situation that is challenging and/or unfamiliar. Sometimes referred to as *what to do when they don't know what to do*, the will of aspiring leaders often drives them to persist to complete a task or meet a challenge. It's their innate talent or fallback strength that's served them well before. For some, it's expertly calming the waters of a contentious conversation by honoring all perspectives while making an executive decision. For others, the will might be strategic studying of data to arrive at the best next step. We've found that the will is connected to the person's interests, and that is why it's so fruitful to discover the passions that drive them. From there, we can develop opportunities where leaders are encouraged to grow their capacities. The development of the will of the leader will be further developed in the next chapter through mentorship.

FIGURE 3.4 LEADERSHIP CONVERSATIONS

PRINCIPAL QUESTION	RESPONSE	FOLLOW-UP QUESTION
Tell me what you know about our leadership standards.	*I am aware they exist on our district webpage and have had exposure to them. While I don't know them off by heart, I have them printed in my office.*	Perfect; which standards might be more aligned with your previous roles and which may need a bit more explanation?
What leadership experiences did you engage in at your school site?	*I had a lot of responsibilities, but mainly I was responsible for leading staff-level meetings. Our school was a K–9 school, and I was the assistant principal for the 7–9 cohort. I was their main point of contact and led their cohort staff meetings.*	What might be some experiences you would like more exposure to? What are some experiences you may want to continue to develop?
What are some of your leadership experiences from outside school?	*I actually own a business on the side of this job with my partner. Together we run a food truck business that employs five people. My role is to manage employees and payroll.*	Amazing! How do you think this experience may help you in your role as a principal?

WHAT ARE YOUR LEADERSHIP STRENGTHS?

Consider this. Sometimes we have our own personal blind spots and may not be aware of some of our strengths and dispositions. Luckily, there are countless leadership personality tests online.

One way to determine your dispositions and those of your leadership team would be to take one of these quizzes and discuss your findings. We suggest giving the high5test a try. You can find the free online test at high5test.com. We have also included a QR code for you to access the online test from a mobile device.

Here are some questions for reflection that you and your leadership team can discuss:

- Which dispositions surprised you the most as being your strength?

- Which dispositions did you think would be your strongest, but they were not?

- Are there any dispositions that were not labeled as strengths that you would like to develop further?

- Which dispositions may need to be developed to best support your school/community?

Thrill

The will is the steely strength—the thrill is the action. The energy of executing one's knowledge and will. Developing the thrill of leadership requires us to design an environment that is not only exciting but also provides the opportunity for our aspiring leader to take action. In this way, they accrue sufficient practical leadership experiences. Motivation can only be developed when a person experiences a degree of efficacy that sparks the desire to continue learning and leading. Thus, we must use the environment in which we are fostering leadership and consider how we may offer opportunities for leaders to experience the thrill of leadership.

> *Motivation can only be developed when a person experiences a degree of efficacy that sparks the desire to continue learning and leading.*

Taken together, the skill, will, and thrill comprise a person's sense of self-efficacy. Later in the chapter we will unpack an example of learning about "where our leaders are" when we share aspects of the methodology used by Cusack (2020) in undertaking the self-efficacy of assistant principals. This will help solidify the impact we can have by taking time to engage in the process of knowing what prior leadership experiences our current assistant principals have had. For now, we recommend taking a few minutes to pause and ponder with the following reflection question.

ROOTED REFLECTION

Based on the definitions of the skill, will, and thrill of leadership what strategies might you implement to gain a better understanding of where your aspiring leaders are in their leadership development?

Discern Affective State

If we are to help assistant principals better mobilize the motivation, cognitive resources, and courses of action needed to meet situational demands of their leadership role, we need to understand their affective state. Affective state (also known as physiological arousal) is central to the understanding of how a person's behavior may be influenced by internal thoughts and beliefs and by the environment including other individuals. Our feelings and mood can bias how and what we think. This in turn can have a profound impact on our sense of self-efficacy. We know that positive moods activate thoughts of previous accomplishments, whereas negative moods precipitate thoughts of past failures. Thus, our affective state can influence how events are interpreted, cognitively stored, and retrieved.

Additionally, our mood can bias affective and cognitive processes and shape perceptions of our self-efficacy. "Those of high efficacy expect to gain favorable outcomes through good performance, whereas those who expect poor performances of themselves conjure up negative outcomes" (Bandura, 2009, p. 180). Understanding where your aspiring leaders are in terms of their dispositions (affective state) is vital to determining what conditions in the school (or jurisdictional) environment and culture need to be addressed or receive greater attention. This ultimately shapes perceptions of self-efficacy.

> *Those of high-efficacy expect to gain favorable outcomes through good performance, whereas those who expect poor performances of themselves conjure up negative outcomes. (Bandura, 2009, p. 180)*

ROOTED REFLECTION

Think about the emotions, feelings, ideas, and attitudes you held when you first became an assistant principal (principal or systems leader). Were you nervous? Excited? Pumped? Terrified? Confident? Make a list of the positive and /or negative feelings you had at the time. How did you overcome any feelings of stress or anxiety you may have had?

Realizing that we all bring our affective state with us wherever we go enriches our work, for we are more mindful of our need to adapt the support as needed. As systems leaders, we need to help aspiring leaders navigate the churn of uncertainty and point the bow of our ship of affective state so to speak, into the waves of self-efficacy. Remember, taking time to learn about the *who* behind the leader prior to engaging in the *what* of leadership is really what understanding affective state is about. Getting to the *what* can be enhanced via the next factor of Social Cognitive Learning Theory (SCLT): social persuasion.

Leverage Social Persuasion

If we think about how we learn, it is largely through the combination of observing and then attempting the task. We watch someone perform a task and make a determination if we might be able to do what they are doing. If the task seems too complex, difficult, or causes discomfort, it is quite likely that we might try to avoid that particular task or situation. We know that fight, flight, or freeze are inherent to human response. We also know, however, that words of encouragement (a pep talk), guidance, and clarifying expectation can be helpful in nudging a person from thinking about doing something to the actual doing.

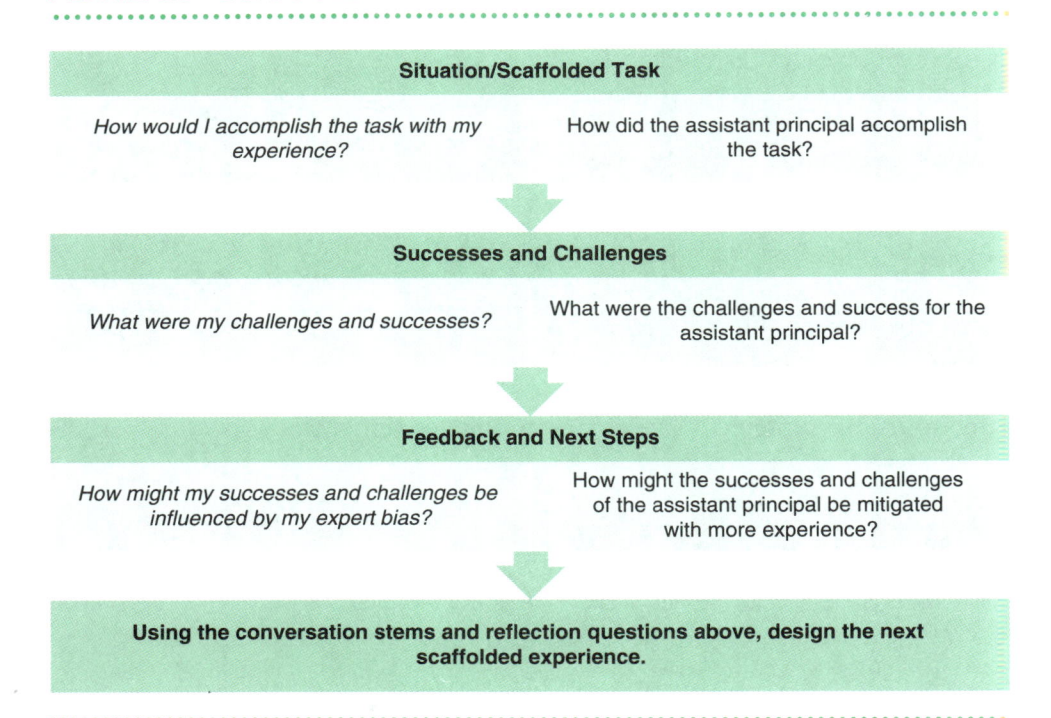

FIGURE 3.5 SCAFFOLDED REFLECTION

Situation/Scaffolded Task

How would I accomplish the task with my experience?

How did the assistant principal accomplish the task?

↓

Successes and Challenges

What were my challenges and successes?

What were the challenges and success for the assistant principal?

↓

Feedback and Next Steps

How might my successes and challenges be influenced by my expert bias?

How might the successes and challenges of the assistant principal be mitigated with more experience?

↓

Using the conversation stems and reflection questions above, design the next scaffolded experience.

How to Scaffold

Is there a recent situation with an assistant principal when you noticed them faltering and used language to support their success? Or, what happens when you want an assistant principal to try and undertake a new and novel task? How might you reword or clarify the expectation? Can your expectation be broken down into do-able steps? Naming the steps of a strategy or action you want them to do can be helpful. How do you scaffold their work? Using a combination of feedback on what they are doing well and reminders of the steps of the process might be the best way to encourage taking a risk. Keeping in mind that we are the leader with more experience, we have to scaffold our expectations of our assistant principals as well. Shedding our *expert bias* and leading empathetically will allow for a greater learning experience for our aspiring leaders. Have a look at the flowchart in Figure 3.5 that will allow for reflection and conversation between your aspiring leader and yourself.

How to Calm

Sometimes social persuasion requires us to focus on **calming** the anxious, **cautioning** the overzealous like those who might want to jump into new situations both feet first, and **counseling** others to perhaps consider an alternative pathway. First, ask yourself:

- What is your comfort level with gently stepping in with advice for an assistant principal who needs to slow down and reflect before acting?

- Is there something you can take off their plate? An initiative that isn't crucial?

- What techniques do you use to help a colleague who is overly emotional about something cool down enough to apply more reason?

Thus, social persuasion pertains to the ability to encourage, motivate, or convince someone to come out of their comfort zone or conversely, to take time to self-reflect before entering into a new situation.

Helpful Ways to Leverage Social Persuasion

When we recall the various rationales provided by assistant principals who are unsure of their future endeavors, we quickly realize that there are many aspects of becoming a principal that need to be further explored. Imagine if we could convert all the "cup-half-empty" dispositions to "cup-half-full"—we'd head off the impending leader shortage! That said, sometimes social persuasion is about talking people out of things (out-counseling) as much as it can be to encourage moving forward. There will always be some trainees who are best dissuaded from pursuing leadership; an optimal leadership development environment acknowledges that care-frontations are always better than confrontations. These conversations require trust (which we will explore fully in the next chapter). Figure 3.6 presents the areas of assistant principal efficacy that we found to be most prevalent and offers corresponding meditative questions that could be leveraged to facilitate the conversations and care-frontations needed.

> *An optimal leadership development environment acknowledges that care-frontations are always better than confrontations.*

Tailor Feedback

We cultivate leadership effectively when we know the type of feedback an individual responds to best regarding a specific task. Individuals who are persuaded (or convinced) about the efficacy of their skills, accept more responsibility, expend greater effort, and have higher accountability for the outcomes of their actions: positive or negative.

The knowledge and credibility of the person offering feedback, weighed against the receiver's confidence in his or her self-appraisal, can positively increase levels of self-efficacy. This is an important concept for principals and systems leaders to take to heart! Skilled efficacy builders do more than give inspirational pep talks; they structure activities that foster success and encourage people to think of success in terms of self-improvement as opposed to outperforming others. Meditative questions are a tool that can be used to leverage feedback and determine the feelings of our aspiring leaders. We like

FIGURE 3.6 SELF-EFFICACY CONVERSATION STARTERS

GENERAL CONCERNS OR COMMENTS	MEDITATIVE QUESTIONS TO ASK ASPIRING PRINCIPALS AS A FOLLOW-UP
• The role of principal is too challenging or too complex • The role of principal is too stressful or too demanding • Increased central office demands on the role	• What aspects of being a principal do you feel are most challenging? • What are your wonderings about the supports in place for principals? • In your current role, what are your challenges and what do you feel would be helpful in supporting you? • What might central leadership do to better support principals?
• I enjoy my current role and am content to stay • I need more time to consider my next steps	• What aspect of being a principal would excite you the most? • What additional opportunities do you think would be helpful in preparing you for a possible next step? • How might your current years of service and experience benefit a new learning community?
• I worry about family (work/life balance)	• What support do you think would be helpful for your work/life needs moving forward? • How might your school or the division assist you?
• I am frustrated within my current position/role	• How might we better define or communicate the expectations of your role? • How would you suggest central leadership further support you in your role?
• I am not sure if I will remain in education field	• What opportunities, supports, or environmental factors do you feel would help you remain in school leadership?

to use meditative questions to dig deeper into the potential concerns of becoming a principal and unearth some additional information that will allow us to better guide and understand the next steps of development (Figure 3.6 .

MEASURING SELF-EFFICACY

Now that we've established that determining our assistant principals' affective state and social persuasion fosters growth, the lingering question remains: How might we measure the self-efficacy of assistant principals?

ROOTED REFLECTION

1. How do we know where our assistant principals are in terms of their self-efficacy? How do we currently measure this? If we do not measure this, how might we start?

2. How is social persuasion layered into your assistant principal development programming?

It is the first day of the new school year for first year assistant principal Anna Newshom at Point West Academy School. Anna is joining an already-established leadership team that has a veteran assistant principal and school leader (principal) Whitney Vista. The first two weeks of the year are dedicated for leadership preparation and establishing norms and routines prior to teachers and students returning for the new year. Today is the first official encounter between Anna and Whitney.

Other than her teaching and instructional coach resume, Whitney does not know much about Anna's leadership experience, so day one is dedicated to building a professional relationship. The purpose of today is to learn more about Anna as a leader.

"So, tell me about yourself and your leadership in schools," Whitney begins. Anna proceeds to tell her about the focus of her master's thesis on instructional leadership, her experiences as a department chair, and her role in the implementation of new curriculum and resources at her previous site. The conversation moves positively and productively, but Anna is shocked when Whitney follows up with a second question. "That is brilliant! Now tell me about your leadership experiences and passions outside of a school environment." This is a question that Anna has never been asked, so naturally she replies, "I'd love to, but I am just curious why you asked this question?"

Whitney explains to Anna that leadership experiences outside of the school context are exceptionally important as they tend to develop other skills and motivations that are not always prevalent in school-specific environments. She continues "it is important for me to know all about you. Your passions, experiences, and knowledge make you the leader you are today, and knowing those things about you will allow me to better develop your leadership capacity."

Anna explains about her leadership roles outside of the school and how she feels they could be best deployed and developed at Point West Academy. Her experiences as a volunteer with a local charity as their president could lead to a wonderful community collaboration with the school. Upon the conclusion of the meeting, Anna is feeling very good about working as an assistant principal. Especially knowing that her principal is actively seeking out to learn more about her as a professional and a person.

UNPACKING CUSACK'S (2020) FINDINGS

Over the course of my research, I (Tim) attempted to determine what led to higher and lower levels of self-efficacy with assistant principals, using a Principal Sense of Efficacy Scale (PSES) survey tool. Here is a quick summary of my findings. We have included a more detailed description of the research, including strategies to measure self-efficacy and a link to detailed findings in the appendix (Figure 3.7).

WHAT WE WANTED TO KNOW	WHAT THE ASSISTANT PRINCIPALS SAID
What percentage of assistant principals held aspirations to become principal?	No = 21% Undecided = 44% Yes = 35%
What was the top reason for saying yes, no, or being undecided?	No: Role is too complex and demanding Undecided: Role is too complex and demanding Yes: Statements about having ability/self-efficacy/ strengths
Which overall areas of leadership (instructional, managerial, and ethical) would have the highest levels of reported self-efficacy?	Moral/ethical was rated highest Instructional was next for all groups Managerial was the lowest level of all groups
What might assistant principals suggest were the top areas of need in terms of their professional learning?	No: More mentorship and distributive leadership opportunities Undecided: More mentorship and guided opportunities to learn Yes: School operations (finances) and more mentoring opportunities

What We Noticed

When we think about self-efficacy beliefs, Bandura (2009) reminds us that "those of high efficacy expect to gain favorable outcomes through good performance, whereas those who expect poor performances of themselves conjure up negative outcomes" (p. 180). This is important because when we look at the language choices of those who said no or who were undecided about becoming principals, we sense a reluctance or hesitance to commit because of affective perceptions that the role is too stressful or challenging. In a way, these respondents are talking themselves out of taking the next step. This becomes somewhat a self-fulfilling prophecy versus an opportunity to increase self-efficacy, which is why it is fundamental for us as leaders to understand and react to the perceptions of self-efficacy in our aspiring leaders. Consider the following voice from a principal who has made it a mission to mentor and coach her aspiring leaders as they grow themselves in their leadership capacity.

LISTENING TO THE VOICE OF PRINCIPAL TONI WOODS

Rio Vista Elementary School, San Bernardino, California

The principal leadership role has shifted from a management role to an instructional leadership role over the past two decades. In my 12 years as a site-level principal, I have found it essential to have the "right" person leading alongside the principal to ensure effective instruction throughout the school day and beyond. During my tenure, I have had either one or two assistant principals, but I am currently the only administrator at my school. Whether I have had an assistant principal or not, I believe it is essential to impart the knowledge and practices necessary for willing staff members to assume the role of leader effectively.

I have coached up teachers from the classroom and assistant principals to principal positions over the course of my career. It is essential to develop the skills and knowledge of the potential future site leaders on your campus. Teacher feedback/coaching, delivering professional development, and creating systems that involve other staff members for effective implementation are the primary areas on which I concentrate.

In my first year as a principal, I began developing teachers for leadership positions. Despite the fact that they were not assistant principals, I quickly observed their will, skill, and thrill in their daily work. I recall asking one of my fourth-grade teachers why she was still in the classroom after observing her instructional practices, relationships with her students, and interactions with her colleagues. She explained that the previous principal discussed her moving to a support teacher position but lacked the necessary funding. At that point, I made it a priority to determine how to remove this teacher from the classroom so she could expand her knowledge and development in a broader leadership capacity. The subsequent year, I did exactly that. During her three years in a support role, she performed coaching cycles with teachers who needed instructional support, provided professional development to our certificated staff, developed technology implementation systems and MTSS monitoring systems, and acted as a true support for all classroom teachers. After three years, she was prepared for the role of assistant principal. She quickly rose to the position of site principal as a result of her tremendous success in that role. Providing her with the opportunity to expand her skill set and not only embrace the excitement of leadership but also instill it in others gave her the tools she needed to be a successful site leader.

It is essential for all site leaders to provide opportunities for future site leaders to develop their skills. When you encounter staff members with the desire and enthusiasm to become educational leaders of the future, it is your responsibility to help them develop their skills.

THE CULTURE FOR IMPLEMENTATION

In this chapter we have discussed how to create a culture for implementation that satisfies the Universal Leadership Standards (ULSs) of *community and culture*. It almost goes without saying that a community that fosters leadership development will have dramatic impacts on leadership experiences. It's the proverbial win-win of a healthy community; everyone from students to leaders thrive.

We have also explored how having a sense of the affective state of our assistant principals allows us to mentor. We can better understand where they are and therefore gauge their sense of self-efficacy. The skill, will, and thrill of our future leaders must be considered as we move forward with the construction of leadership learning experiences. Knowing more about *who* the aspiring leader is will result in more deliberate planning and implementation of leadership development. A survey tool such as the ULS tool or PSES can be helpful; yet, if you are already using a tool to gather information, that is great. What we wanted to impart is that gathering rich data from open-ended questions about what your assistant principals are currently experiencing and what they feel is needed to help them is also critically important. Knowing that the central leaders and school principals want to create great learning conditions is at the root of the level of trust needed for successful implementation. Encouraging an environment that is built in consideration of the skill, will, and thrill of leadership as well as the self-efficacy of aspiring leaders are the key driving factors for leadership development.

SYSTEMS CHECK

In seeking to better understand the importance of creating an environment conducive to supporting stronger leadership development, let's pause and consider the following questions.

1. Use Appendix 3, the UL inventory, to determine the reported sense of efficacy of your assistant principals across the four domains: Learning and Engagement, Resources and Operations, Community and Culture, and Growth and Innovation. Where is there strength? What needs improvement?

2. What are the differences in perspectives of leadership skill, will, and thrill across the various levels of leadership within your jurisdiction or school? Are all stakeholders at a similar level of understanding?

3. To what extent, if any, do differences in reported self-efficacy exist across such demographics as gender, years of teaching experience, years of administrative experience, level of education, level of school (e.g., elementary or secondary), and amount of teaching assignments as assistant principals?

4. If you were to sit down individually with Sammi, Doug, and Gemma (our assistant principals from earlier in this chapter), what words of advice or wisdom would you share in seeking to increase their sense of self-efficacy?

IMPLEMENTATION POINTS TO PONDER

Consider using similar research questions as Cusack (2020) in terms of how the information you glean might help inform where your assistant principals are in terms of their attitudes and disposition toward principalship.

1. Determine what prior teacher leader roles your current assistant principals held prior to becoming a formal school leader (e.g., learning coach, department head, counselor, consultant, etc.). Are there any teacher leader roles presenting with higher levels of reported self-efficacy over others? If so, what might explain the difference?

2. Determine how many assistant principals aspire for principalship and what professional learning experiences opportunities they suggest are needed in terms of becoming a principal. This will give you rich insights into the attitudes and dispositions (affective state) of your people. It will also inform the conversations needed (social persuasion) to further create the environmental conditions most conducive to growth.

PREDICTIVE INQUIRY

Use the following table to compare your predictions with the content presented in this chapter.

CREATING A CULTURE FOR IMPLEMENTATION	
Predictions that were correct:	Questions I still have:
New information learned:	

CHAPTER 4

PLANNING GUIDED LEADERSHIP EXPERIENCES

You cannot transmit wisdom and insight to another person. The seed is already there. A good teacher touches the seed, allowing it to wake up, to sprout, and to grow.

—*Thich Nhat Hanh*

FOUR ROOTS OF SCHOOL LEADER PREPARATION

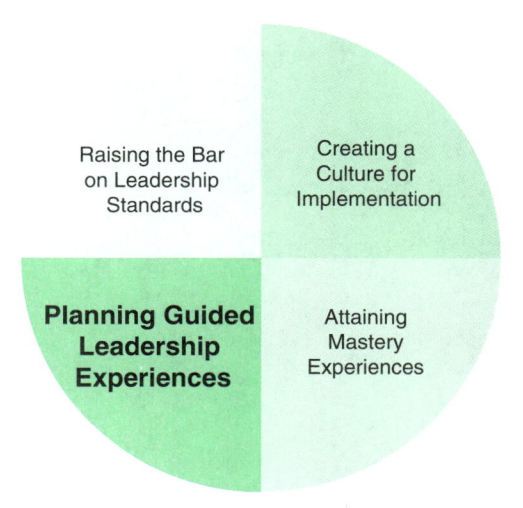

When we think of the adage *just as you sow; you shall reap*, we realize that the energy, effort, and time we put into an endeavor, minimally, are what we hope to get out of it. Yet often, we hear about "the principal pipeline" as a solution to addressing the shortage of school leaders. We've always found that an inelegant metaphor; put oil, water, gas, or any other commodity into a pipeline at one end and that is exactly what you get at the terminus. What is in the pipeline hasn't changed in any way. That's not what leadership development is. Yes, we want a steady flow of new talent, but that's where the analogy ends. As we explored in the previous chapters, our model is grounded in research and best practices of standards, but it is pliant. It bends to the direction of each person's professional passions and particular strengths; in short, their skill, will, and thrill.

UNIVERSAL LEADERSHIP STANDARDS FOCUS

Growth and Innovation: This leadership standard reflects all capacities of continuous growth and systems excellence. This includes promoting opportunities for ongoing growth for all stakeholders. Leaders who focus on this standard create conditions for innovation and creativity through an environment that embraces risk-taking and experiential learning.

Resources and Operations: This leadership standard reflects all capacities of managerial and adherence to state regulations or legislation. This may include decisions involving the deployment of finances, human capital, materials, and infrastructure to best support the learning community.

Learning and Engagement: This leadership standard reflects all capacities of instructional leadership. This may include decisions that directly impact the students, staff, and community stakeholders. Leaders who implement this standard acknowledge the impact of high-quality instruction on student learning and achievement.

WHAT DO WE KNOW ABOUT GUIDED EXPERIENCE?

We want our school leaders to weather the strong winds of administrative challenges that arise time and again. To do this, we need to intentionally guide them. Let's begin by defining what we mean by guided experience, which includes vicarious learning experiences, and how this operates within leadership development.

We learn by first observing others. A vicarious experience is one in which learning is a result of the direct observation or modeling of others (e.g., a mentor or coach). We experience the skill vicariously through watching an expert or more knowledgeable other perform the task we aspire to master. We then reinforce that learning through doing the observed task. This reinforcement is what factors into our understanding of guided leadership experiences. Essentially, humans tend to observe others similar to themselves or whom they perceive to be successful in their job or role. Sometimes it simply equates to watching someone else and determining "if they can do it, I can do it." In our quest to learn, each individual brings their own mix of doubt and self-efficacy. Guided practice allows time for repetition and learning from mistakes. Guided learning articulates the steps needed to increase learner efficacy and move toward mastery. Self-efficacy, particularly in the area of vicarious and guided experiences, can influence

- which behavior(s) the observer might seek to emulate,
- how much effort will be expended in replicating the behavior,
- perseverance in facing obstacles and failure,
- level of resiliency during difficulties,
- if thought patterns and processes (such as self-talk) are self-aiding or self-hindering, and
- how well stress is or is not managed (coping skills) in light of the environmental context.

Think back to the voices from the field in Chapter 3 and how striking it was to notice the differences in disposition between them. To put it simply, some people come to the table with greater confidence in the face of uncertainty than others. As we explored in the previous chapter, we can lessen the anxiety—and drop-out rate of aspiring principals—by understanding their dispositions (their will). What we know about their will can help us establish an understanding and specific direction of their potential leadership.

In this chapter, we continue this journey by exploring a Levels of Experience Model that shows a progression from a novice level of learner toward mastery levels of understanding. First, we will discuss how critical it is for leaders to be trustworthy. Why? Trust is a key ingredient in creating an environment conducive to growth and the corresponding learning experiences that are essential for assistant principal development. In order to guide an aspiring leader along the pathway, trust is central to any and all work we do in education.

ROOTED REFLECTION

Consider this statement: "People with high assurance in their capabilities approach difficult tasks as challenges to be mastered rather than as threats to be avoided" (Bandura, 1977, p. 11). Does this ring true for you?

PROGRESSIONS OF EXPERIENCES

Leadership standards outline the competencies essential to the role and responsibilities of school leadership. We quickly realize that there are numerous skills, criteria, and indicators of performance to address. How we set out to provide the necessary experiences to address the competencies is at the heart of creating guided leadership experiences. We propose a graduated model of experiences. The professional learning of an aspiring leader takes them from less challenging experiences to more complex responsibilities. We illustrate these intentional progressions in Figure 4.1.

Notice that there is a leadership standard at the base of this graphic. As we explored in Chapter 2, standards root all of our work in agreed-upon skills, goals, and values. Standards give us a common language to use in every vicarious and guided learning experience. The standards are the words that inform the metacognitive thinking; the standards are the currency of communication in every discussion, providing legitimacy and benchmarks. Without this foundation, there may be a perception that the experience is just occurring by happenstance. We want to ensure aspiring leaders are aware that these experiences are being deliberately created by design.

As you design guided leadership experiences, you'll want to plan them so they increase in complexity. We like to literally label them as Levels one–three to better ensure we are building in greater and greater degrees of responsibility for the aspiring leader.

FIGURE 4.1 LEVELS OF LEADERSHIP EXPERIENCE

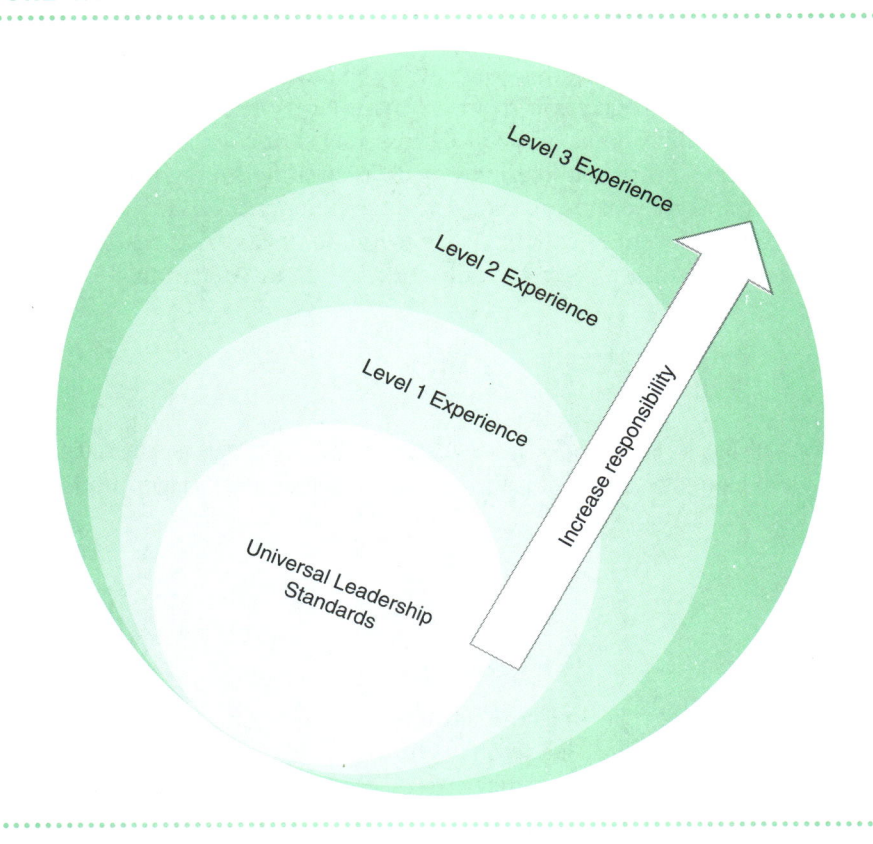

Level 1 Experiences: The first vicarious experience should involve the aspiring leader in a more limited capacity (observation, passive involvement, self-reflection, etc.) in which the goal should be that they become familiar and comfortable with the leadership task. In this experience, the leader (mentor) should be modeling expected behaviors and being receptive to questions from the aspiring leader. Moving through the next two levels of experiences requires the mentor to determine when the aspiring leader is ready to take more responsibility.

Level 2 Experiences: The next phase is often conducted in partnership with both leader and aspiring leader taking action and responsibility. The key attribute of the second guided experience is that the aspiring leader must be responsible for a deliverable, meaning they have independent responsibility for a certain aspect of the leadership experience.

Level 3 Experiences: The last experience level is where we should expect the aspiring leader to take complete control and responsibility. The mentor/leader should act as a guide and support as the aspiring leader navigates their way through the leadership experience independently. That is not to say the leader should not be present for this part of the guided experience but rather should provide a comfortable opportunity for the development of the aspiring leader. By letting the aspiring leader know they are there in case they are needed, this last leadership experience can be the most fruitful when it comes to the development of the skill or disposition of the aspiring leader.

We do not want to downplay the importance of time as a measurement of readiness as well. Certain aspiring leaders will need more time with each experience level prior to moving to the next stage. This will naturally be dependent on the mentor to make the appropriate judgment. We will explore the concepts of mastery experiences in the next chapter, as a means to determine when our aspiring leaders are truly ready for the next steps.

We will soon provide some examples of how to navigate the circles of responsibility using the Universal Leadership Standards from our previous chapter. Until then, we welcome you to consider the following Rooted Reflection.

ROOTED REFLECTION

Think about your own development as an aspiring leader. What opportunities to experience increasing degrees of responsibility did you receive? What does this look like today for the aspiring leaders in your jurisdiction?

MOVING FROM GUIDED TO MASTERY LEARNING EXPERIENCES

The three levels of experiences that a leader co-plans with an assistant principal can be many different things. You know your school, the current front-burner issues, initiatives, and events. You know the context of your trainee. Our advice is that you allow your trainee to paint on a broad enough canvas; that is, have them try their hand at communicating and engaging with a vital audience. For example, when we consider the importance of community involvement, especially parent voice in educational decision-making, we know that the principal has a key role to play in fostering strong relationships and a good flow of communication between home and school. School councils (Parent Teacher Associations [PTAs]) are often legally required constructs within the local state. These meetings provide opportunity for parents and guardians to lend their voices to discussions about supporting the school community. The principal is generally required to provide a general overview of school activities and operations. Figure 4.2 examines Community Engagement, which comes under the broader Stewardship of Community and Culture domain. In seeking to provide more meaningful learning experiences for assistant principals, consider the three experiences (one for each of the three levels) depicted in Figure 4.2.

FIGURE 4.2 COMMUNITY AND ENGAGEMENT, LEVELS OF EXPERIENCE

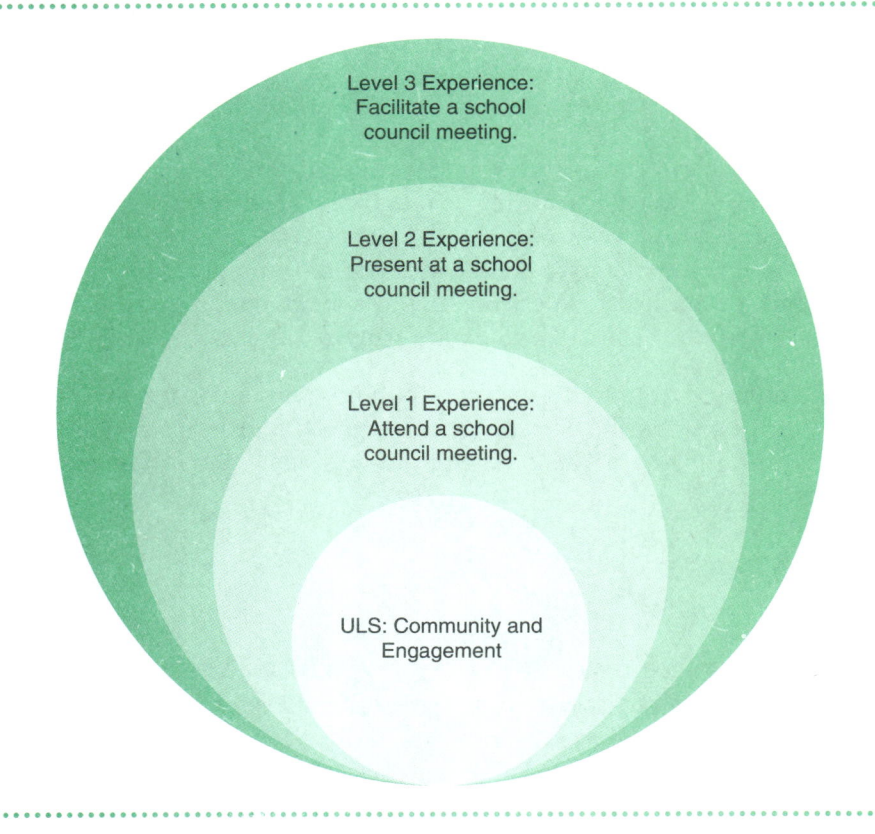

Level 3 Experience: Facilitate a school council meeting.

Level 2 Experience: Present at a school council meeting.

Level 1 Experience: Attend a school council meeting.

ULS: Community and Engagement

Level 1 Experiences provide an opportunity for the assistant principal to simply take in the meeting. The principal could provide an overview of the meeting agenda in advance, suggest some look and listen fors, and offer a debriefing to clarify any questions or wonderings about the meeting that the assistant principal may have.

Level 2 Experiences increase the engagement for the assistant principal through the inclusion of a deliverable. In this instance, the assistant principal might offer an overview of upcoming student leadership events, a field trip, or other school operational–related topic. This increases the rigor of the learning. There is a level of preparedness required and the delivery of the information. This may also include responding to questions from parents or other stakeholders. Following the meeting, the principal would lead a debrief and discuss the successes and areas for growth. Level 2 Experience may be a repeated action over the course of a semester or two providing more opportunities for honing skills and gaining confidence.

Level 3 Experiences are truly an opportunity to experience the full weight of the desired outcome or skillset. Perhaps near the end of the school year, the assistant principal would serve in the capacity of principal and chair the meeting. A debriefing would ensue and successes and areas for growth could be addressed.

In this example, we observe that the assistant principal moves from simple to more complex involvement. There is ample opportunity to observe, ask questions, learn from mistakes, and move toward mastery learning. We will soon explore other examples of the learning experiences that assistant principals (Cusack, 2020) deemed to be of importance. You will note that the examples touch upon all four of our Leadership Standards.

CONSIDERING PERSPECTIVES

Westfield Valley Regional School (WVRS) is a Grade 7–12 school with a student population of 1,200, a staff of 50, and three assistant principals. With an array of programming including Science, Technology, Engineering and Math (STEM), athletic academies, and fine arts, there are many pressures on school budgeting and resource allocation. The school division uses a site-based budgeting process (with central overview and support) and provides frequent training for principals on how to manage school finances.

Given a recent increase in retirements, there is a larger number of new principals in the division. It is noticed that there are increased demands for more central support with budget implementation.

Given that there are three assistant principals at WVRS, the Deputy Superintendent reaches out to Dominic, a veteran principal with 10 years' experience, to ask for some perspectives on how the division might better support the financial skills of aspiring principals. Dominic suggests that the division consider including assistant principals in professional learning associated with budgeting. Central office asks Dominic to assemble a small team and suggest what experiences might be helpful. Dominic connects with other principal colleagues to get some ideas. Furthermore, a survey is sent to assistant principals to gain a sense of what they feel might be important or helpful in learning about school financial operations. Finally, central financial services staff are engaged to learn perspectives of current processes and what might be value added should assistant principals be added to training programming.

Here is a series of professional learning activities that were suggested to the central school leadership team from the feedback gathered by Dominic and team members. Dominic and his team are now tasked with determining the most effective order to deliver this professional learning series.

A. Assistant principals will have the opportunity to manage the budgeting of a focus area within the school, for example, athletic academy, fine arts programming, and academic focus program.

B. All assistant principals will be granted read-only access to the school budget workbook (financial records).

C. Assistant principals will have scheduled budget workshop professional development (PD) session with an experienced principal and designated central office financial staff.

D. Assistant principals will be able to make changes in the budget workbook and update sections relevant to their portfolio.

E. Assistant principals will attend a school board meeting at which the division budget is approved.

F. Assistant principals will speak to aspects of the school budget at a parent council (PTA) meeting.

G. Assistant principals will prepare a mock budget and submit to principal or divisional financial staff for peer review.

H. Assistant principals will read state literature pertaining to school funding frameworks and allocations.

I. Assistant principals will co-lead staff discussion on budget planning with the whole staff.

J. Assistant principals will review the school budget workbook to find potential errors, find efficiencies, or make recommendations to the principal.

ACTIVITY 4.1

Place yourself as a member on Dominic's leadership team. Your task is to examine the list of suggested professional learning activities and to organize them by experience level on the Levels of Experiences template which you can find in Activity 4.2 and Appendix 4. What activities might fall into Level of Experience 1, 2, or 3?

After you have completed this activity, see page 74 to read which Level of Experience we suggest for each of these activities.

LISTENING TO THE VOICE OF NICOLE THOMLINSON

K-6 Elementary Principal, École Bishop Savaryn, Edmonton Catholic School Division

I had the pleasure of being an assistant principal for four years with three different principals. Throughout the four years, I experienced a significant shift in assistant principal training to target the development of leadership skills and the preparation for principalship at the divisional level. Learning experiences transferred from passive to purposeful engagement. When I first began as an assistant principal, division formation sessions were rarely aligned with principal meetings and development opportunities. Professional development sessions offered to assistant principals were vague and broad-based. By the time I completed my third year, division training and professional development evolved to build capacity and leadership skills by aligning and involving the assistant principal with principal meetings and formation. I gained access to the workbook and was involved in budgetary discussions, attended principal meetings and development sessions, planned staff engagement discussions regarding the school growth plan, and actively participated in the staffing cycle. Including and valuing assistant principals at the divisional level increased my perceived self-efficacy and experiential learning opportunities. I gained a deeper understanding and respect for the principal role because the admin team worked within a common framework, which at its center, focused on leadership standards, created an environment of trust, and provided learning opportunities that moved us toward mastery learning. Direct insight into the role clarified the expectations and responsibilities involved in a principalship. My leadership journey was enriched by the increased responsibilities entrusted to me.

Unexpectedly, my role changed from assistant principal to principal mid-year. A new assistant principal was assigned to the school, and suddenly, the protégé became the mentor. Navigating new roles and demands proved to be challenging, and time to meet as an administration team was sporadic. I felt that I was not providing the guidance to effectively support the assistant principal and provide the necessary mentorship that I received. The advice shared during a development session also echoed in my mind stating that, as a leader, people will watch you closely. This became apparent when the assistant principal began asking questions about my reaction to different situations. The questions opened the door to conversations about our values, fears, and priorities and provided space for vulnerability. As a result, our newly scheduled Monday morning meetings to review and prioritize tasks also included discussion about the "gray areas" of leadership; the items that arise that cannot be "Googled." This nonnegotiable meeting time allowed for reciprocal learning, constructive conversations, feedback, and reflection. It provided a psychologically safe space rooted in trust for us to discover and develop leadership skills as we discuss how to approach unique situations. Creating intentional time to identify and discuss relevant areas of challenge in our leadership journey has strengthened our interdependence and independence.

SAMPLES OF LEVEL OF EXPERIENCES ALIGNED WITH UNIVERSAL LEADERSHIP STANDARDS

To further illustrate the types of guided to mastery experiences that assistant principals suggested as most helpful (Cusack, 2020), we will now provide some examples from each of our four Universal Leadership Standard (ULS) domains. In each instance you will observe how we move from a surface level of engagement (Level 1 Experiences) and increase the rigor and challenge toward mastery via Level 2 (guided) and Level 3 (mastery) Experiences. We will be looking more specifically at mastery experiences in the next chapter. For now, please note that there are other aspects or elements that could and should be considered in each of the three levels. Your jurisdictional needs may vary; thus, you could readily modify or adapt the examples we will share to best meet your context. Our examples appear in order of most asked for experience (for each standard) from Cusack (2020).

ULS 1: LEARNING AND ENGAGEMENT

FIGURE 4.3   ULS 1: TEACHER SUPERVISION

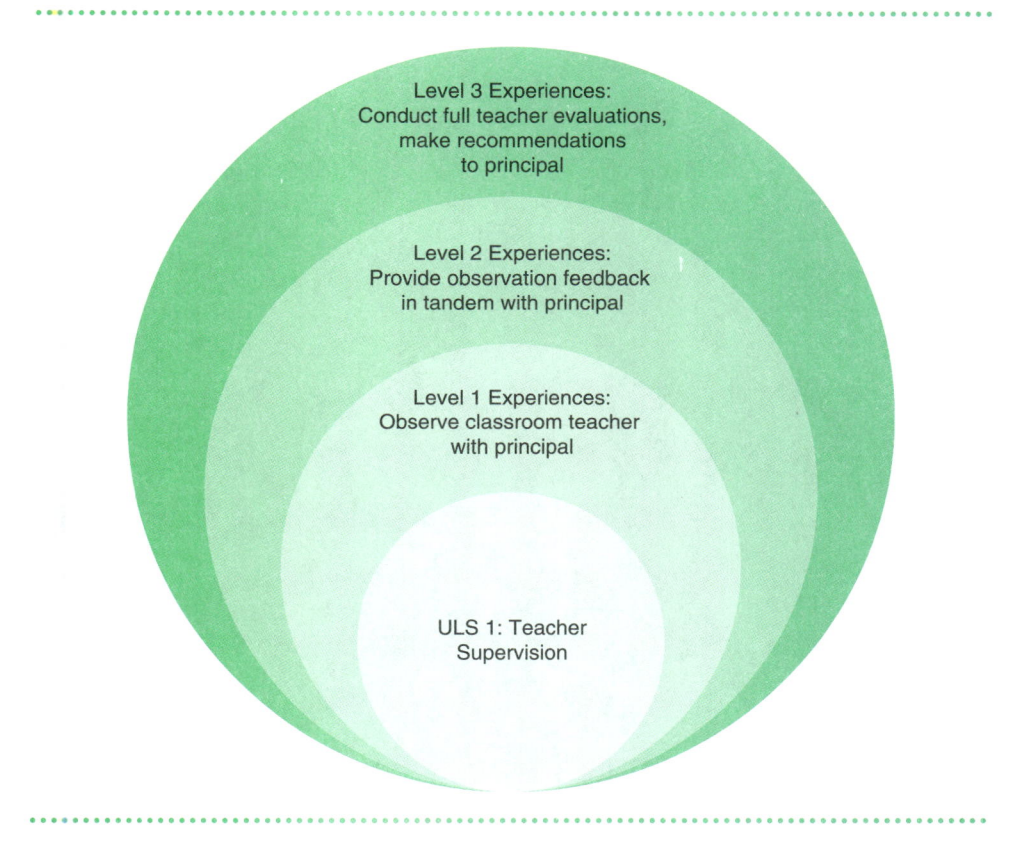

Level 3 Experiences:
Conduct full teacher evaluations,
make recommendations
to principal

Level 2 Experiences:
Provide observation feedback
in tandem with principal

Level 1 Experiences:
Observe classroom teacher
with principal

ULS 1: Teacher
Supervision

FIGURE 4.4 ULS 1: PROFESSIONAL LEARNING OPPORTUNITIES

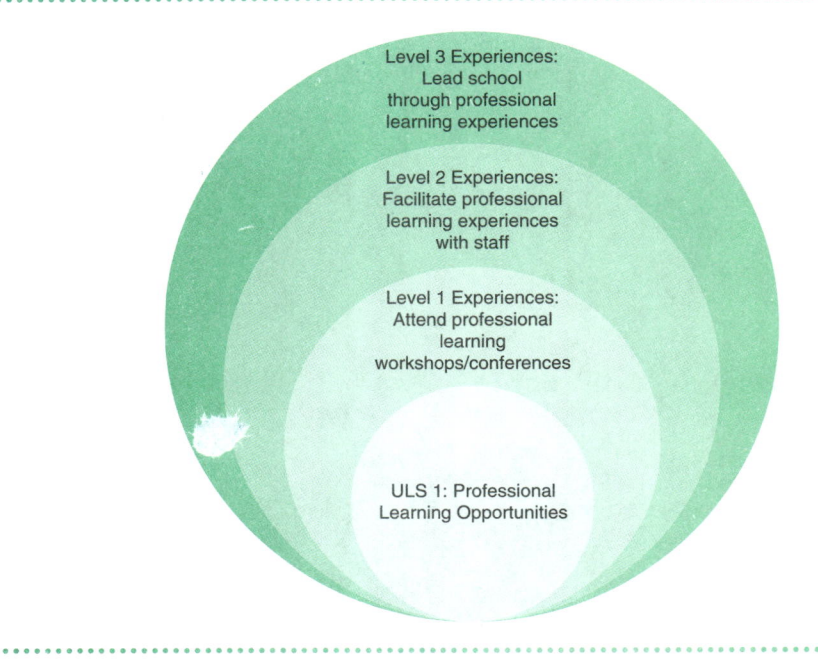

ULS 2: RESOURCES AND OPERATIONS

FIGURE 4.5 ULS 2: SCHOOL BUDGET AND FINANCES

FIGURE 4.6 ULS 2: STAFFING (HR PROCESSES)

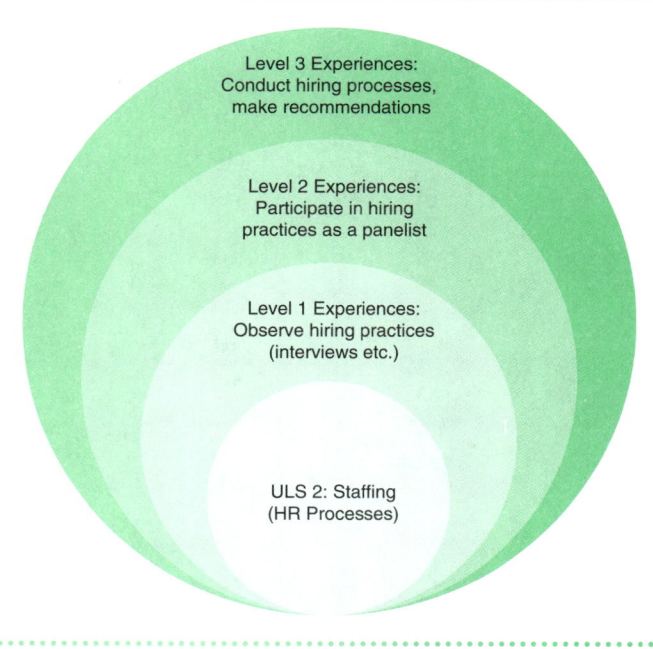

Level 3 Experiences:
Conduct hiring processes,
make recommendations

Level 2 Experiences:
Participate in hiring
practices as a panelist

Level 1 Experiences:
Observe hiring practices
(interviews etc.)

ULS 2: Staffing
(HR Processes)

FIGURE 4.7 ULS 2: EMERGENCY PREPAREDNESS

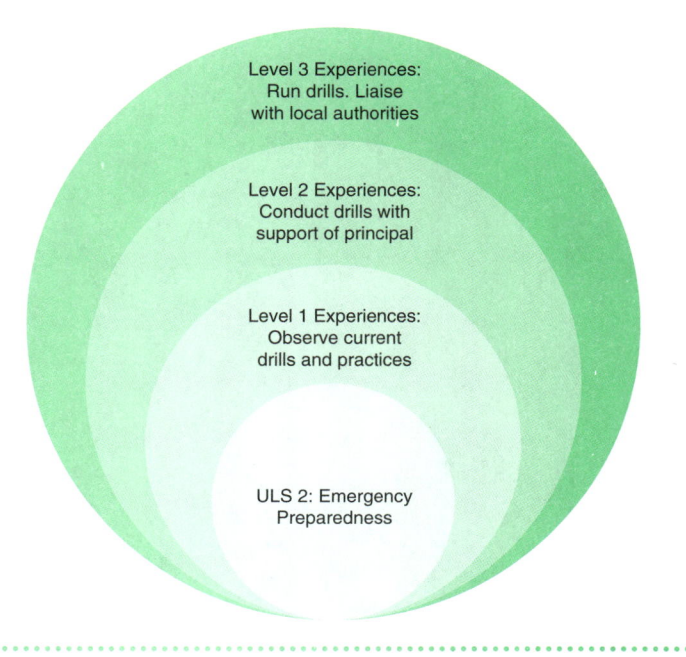

Level 3 Experiences:
Run drills. Liaise
with local authorities

Level 2 Experiences:
Conduct drills with
support of principal

Level 1 Experiences:
Observe current
drills and practices

ULS 2: Emergency
Preparedness

ULS 3: COMMUNITY AND CULTURE

FIGURE 4.8   ULS 3: STAFF ENGAGEMENT

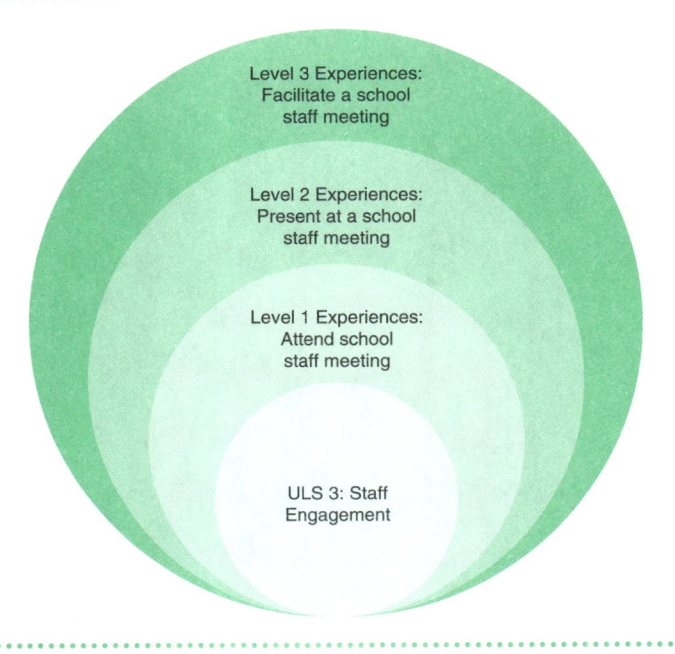

FIGURE 4.9   ULS 3: COMMUNITY ENGAGEMENT

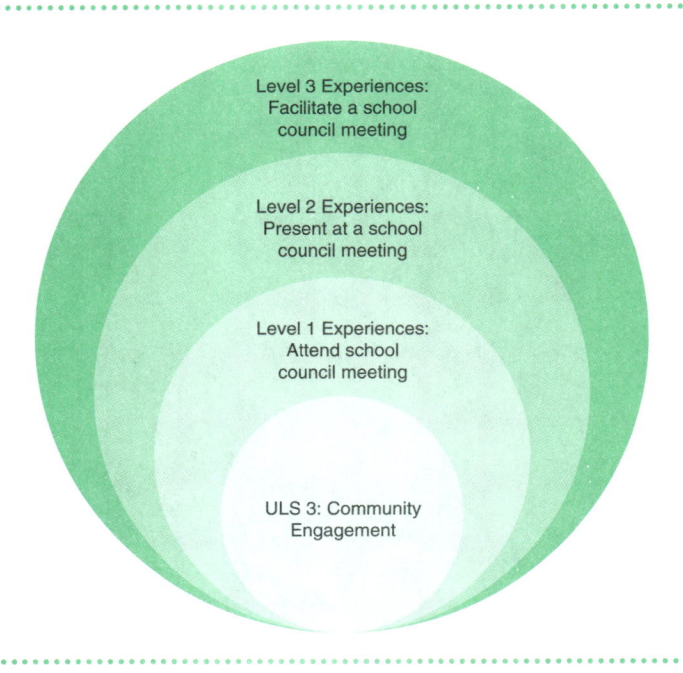

ULS 4: GROWTH AND INNOVATION

FIGURE 4.10   ULS 4: SCHOOL PLAN FOR CONTINUOUS GROWTH

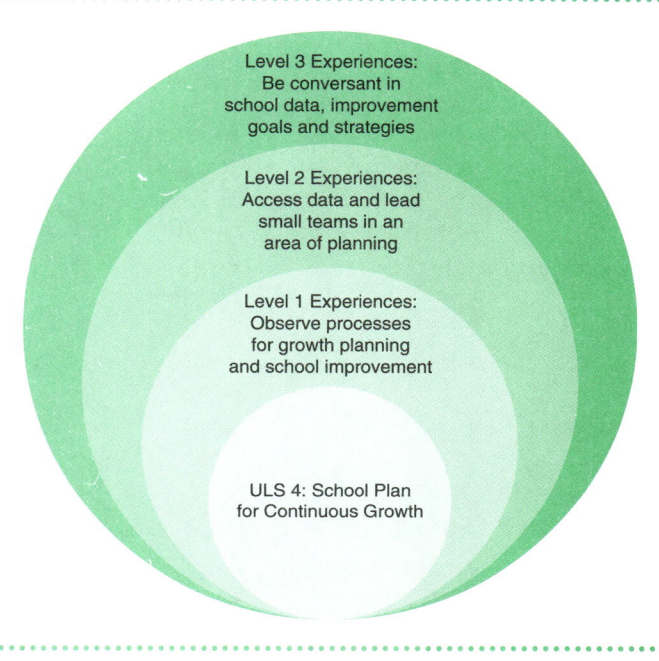

Level 3 Experiences:
Be conversant in
school data, improvement
goals and strategies

Level 2 Experiences:
Access data and lead
small teams in an
area of planning

Level 1 Experiences:
Observe processes
for growth planning
and school improvement

ULS 4: School Plan
for Continuous Growth

FIGURE 4.11   ULS 4: IMPLEMENTATION OF NEW SCHOOL INITIATIVES

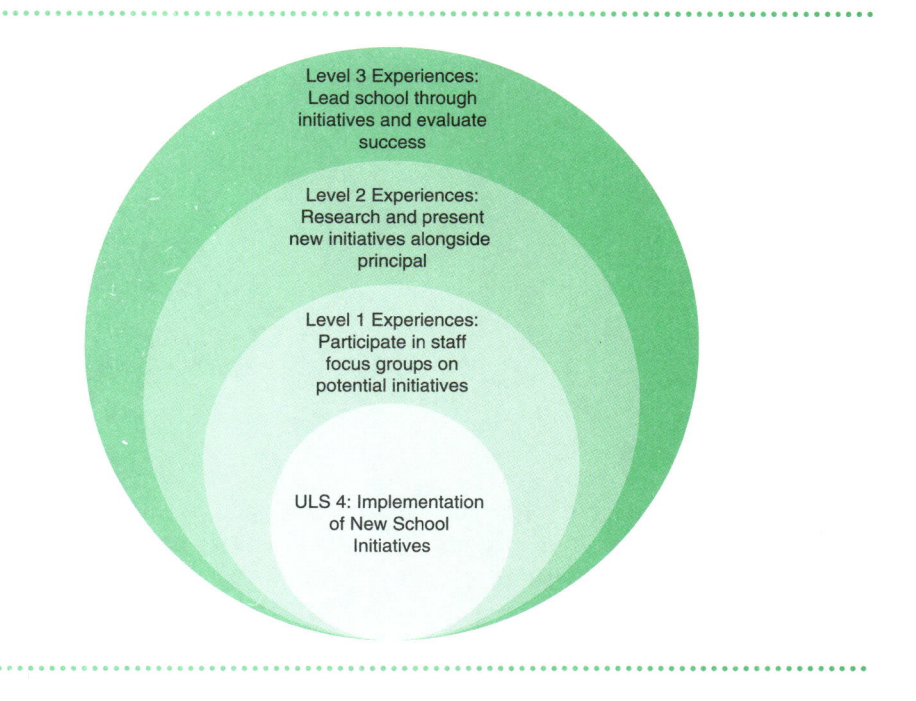

Level 3 Experiences:
Lead school through
initiatives and evaluate
success

Level 2 Experiences:
Research and present
new initiatives alongside
principal

Level 1 Experiences:
Participate in staff
focus groups on
potential initiatives

ULS 4: Implementation
of New School
Initiatives

ACTIVITY 4.2 IDENTIFY LEVELED EXPERIENCES FOR YOUR ASSISTANT PRINCIPALS

Use this blank Levels of Experience template to create leveled experiences in an area of need that you've identified for your assistant principals. Fill in a new template for each area of need you have identified. See also Appendix 4. You can access a printable pdf of this template on this book's resource page at https://us.corwin.com/books/leader-ready-281684.

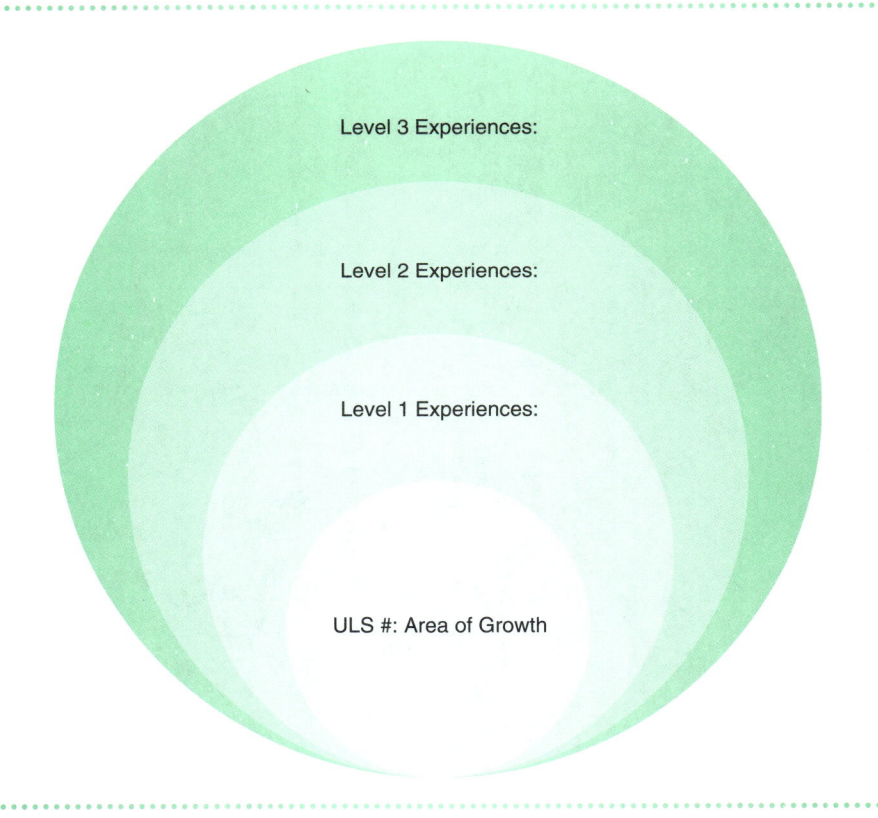

Level 3 Experiences:

Level 2 Experiences:

Level 1 Experiences:

ULS #: Area of Growth

LEADERSHIP DEVELOPMENT AND TRUST

Mentorship and leadership development cannot occur without trust. Over the course of this chapter, we provided what we feel is necessary to establish vicarious and guided learning experiences that are the most impactful for aspiring school leaders. Having trust as the foundation and heart root of guided learning will ensure that leaders feel supported in their development. The mentor's role is to establish trust and an understanding that they are operating in the best interest of their aspiring leader.

How Might We Generate Trust in Our Guided Leadership Experiences?

Trust is a heart root. From botany, we know that a heart root is a large, obliquely descending tree root, as contrasted with a vertical taproot or a horizontal root. In a poetic sense, heart root means a deep connection to all that matters most to a person. It is true that trust is a vital part of an environment where leadership learning takes place. However, we wanted to include a section of behaviors that leaders should be exhibiting as they create guided leadership experiences. Guidance cannot happen without trust; trust cannot be generated without the following actions. We recommend considering how you and other leaders in your organization are demonstrating how to be vulnerable, benevolent, honest, open, and competent.

> *In a poetic sense, heart root means a deep connection to all that matters most to a person.*

BUILDING COLLEGIAL TRUST (MODELED AFTER TSCHANNEN-MORAN & GAREIS, 2015)

Be Vulnerable

The assistant principals observing us are inherently vulnerable because they are just beginning to acquire new skills. To grow, they are going to have to take risks, and perhaps falter and fail. But we need to show our vulnerability too. Often leaders try to do this with "back in the day" stories meant to be instructive, and to convey that they were once newbies too. What our aspiring leaders seek, though, is something else. They want to sense that you are vulnerable in some regards, still inquiring, refining, and slogging through unexpected challenges with grace. When the principal (mentor) models vulnerability, this goes a long way to creating the conditions for that vulnerability to be reciprocated.

As a heart root, collegial trust plays a vital role in helping a leader intuit another's affective state, which in turn helps the leader guide appropriately. This is harder than it sounds! Why? Because if a person shares their deepest feelings about wanting to become a principal, from their inner doubts to their dearest hopes, leaders often meet that candor with superficial cheerleading or suggestions that may have worked for *them* but aren't apt for the trainee. We don't mean to throw all leaders under the bus; we are only trying to bring to light normal human tendencies that get in the way of mentoring. Being vulnerable means putting ourselves far to the side and listening very well so we can support and persuade very well.

Be Benevolent

Benevolence is all about goodness and kindness. For principals and system leaders, benevolence is a call to stewardship. Stewardship involves acts of charity, fairness, kindness, and generosity for others. It includes the inclination to create a safe, caring, and equitable environment.

What are some impactful ways to be benevolent? Here are a few that we think will be helpful:

- Let the assistant principal know that you are committed to supporting them through the experiences and concepts expected for role success. This means being both available and present to the pro·té·gé.

- Be fair but firm in setting expectations for performance. While a good leader should never pass a fault (allow a mistake to go unchecked), correction should be done privately and quietly, always with the dignity of the learner in mind.

- Communicate frequently and via different modes. Verbal and written feedback, record messages, video, notes, etc., should affirm successes and reinforce areas still needing growth.

- As a mentor, know that you must aspire to be a steward and truly be in the service of others. As a servant-leader, the mentor should steady the ladder and let the assistant principal climb.

Benevolence demands that a principal be able to differentiate their intent versus their impact when it comes to the actions they undertake in developing their assistant principal. This is where honesty becomes a game changer.

Be Honest

We know that first impressions can be lasting. If a principal is deemed to be dishonest, it is difficult for that perception to be changed. Statements must match actions. When we hear of the "do as I say but not as I do" type of leadership that exists, we are not likely going to enhance the will, skill, and thrill of aspiring school leaders. When a leader says one thing but does another, when confidentiality is broken, when confidence that a person's work carries weight is compromised, trust does not take root. Honesty requires authenticity. Authenticity means owning the consequences of our words and actions. Assistant Principal, Frederick (in the Listening to the Voices of Assistant Principals section of this chapter) voices a sense of disappointment that he did not receive the development that he expected. In this instance, the authenticity of what was expected versus what was delivered has breached his level of trust (of the principal and jurisdiction) and left Frederick feeling somewhat disillusioned. How can we enhance leadership authenticity so as to increase levels of honesty? Here are a few things known to be helpful for principals:

Authentic leaders

- truthfully represent themselves and their capabilities
- take responsibility for their actions good or bad
- do not shift blame to others
- do not pass the buck, scapegoat, or point fingers at others
- do not leverage positional power to manipulate others
- respect the dignity of all community members
- remove barriers associated with role stereotypes

Be Open

A leader's level of openness (as perceived by staff) is predicated on their ability to communicate. When information is clear, transparent, and frequent, there is a higher likelihood that staff will trust the integrity of both the message and, more importantly, the messenger. Timely feedback, adequate explanations, and engaging the voice of others in decision-making are known to help principal's earn trust.

Having the opportunity for open and honest discussions with their principal and feeling confident that they could share their ideas for school growth and improvement in a trusting environment were important to the assistant principals. The challenge in all this is that often we *think* we are being open and available, but that is not how we are perceived. In our work in schools, we have coached leaders on strategies to make them more open, from asking questions at the outset to smiling more in the hallways to ending any meeting with an assistant principal with a positive comment and a specific, agreed-upon goal. What research tells us, however, is that all that coaching is fine and good, but the surefire way to create openness is to give up control.

Here are a few things you might consider at the system level to enhance this dynamic of being an approachable leader:

- Solicit regular feedback from assistant principals in your division about what types of professional learning they feel is needed.

- Ensure principals know the areas of need and support the principals in being able to deliver that professional learning requested.

- Include assistant principals in professional learning comparable to what principals receive.

- Raise the profile of assistant principals in terms of their inclusion in more jurisdictional strategic planning and visioning.

- Plan professional learning that emphasizes both the theoretical and more so the practical aspects of fostering and deepening the professional trust dynamic between principal and assistant principal.

Be Competent

Competence is the degree to which we are able to perform an expected task or demonstrate a desired outcome. For principals to be effective mentors, this is where the rubber hits the road! Our aspiring school leaders are watching us with wonder and are often hyper aware of every move we make as principals. No different than students in an elementary school classroom who think their teachers are superheroes that live in the classroom, our aspiring leaders are often in awe of the decisions we must make. So, it is exceptionally important to do our job to the best of our abilities, as we set the example for the next principals of our schools. From showing up on time, running meetings efficiently, managing budgets, assisting upset parents to how you treat your support staff, everything we do can have a ripple effect on our perceived competence. When a leader demonstrates capability to perform as expected, staff are more likely to generate a higher level of trust for that leader. If a principal is not viewed as competent, trust is diminished. This is particularly problematic when that principal is serving as a mentor for an aspiring leader.

ROOTED REFLECTION

In what ways do your current leadership development programs address or explore the dynamic of trust between principals and assistant principals? Which aspects of trust do you feel might warrant further exploration or intentionality in your leadership programming?

LISTENING TO THE VOICES OF ASSISTANT PRINCIPALS

To set the stage for our exploration of how guided learning intersects with relational trust, consider the voices and thoughts of Frederick, Kinesha, and Selma.

Frederick (K–6) "In my professional growth plan, I listed a few areas of instructional leadership where I felt I needed to learn more, especially in teacher supervision and evaluations. My principal indicated that we would work on this collaboratively, but I was soon tasked with being school liaison for a major renovation project that our school had to undergo. This meant lots of rescheduling teaching spaces and the moving of desks and materials. When I asked about the plans to help with teacher evaluations, I was told not to worry; we would tend to it next year once the building renovation project would be done. How do I increase my skills as an instructional leader when I was relegated to a building modernization for months on end? I am super frustrated!"

Kinesha (K–9) "I have been blessed to have had experience in six different schools and over fifteen different administrators. I have learned so much about my leadership style from positive and negative examples of their leadership. I want, one day, to take all that I have learned through professional development and experience and lead a staff and school community."

Selma (High School) "I would like to continue to develop my skills and abilities under the mentorship, guidance, and support of an experienced principal. This would allow me the confidence to one day apply for principalship. The thing is, I am not sure my current principal is the best model for me, and I do not know how to address my feelings with my principal."

ROOTED REFLECTION

If you had to assess the level of trust that Frederick, Kinesha, and Selma currently have in terms of their experiences, development, and readiness for principalship, what would you say? What evidence supports your observations? What do you feel is important when it comes to trust?

GUIDED LEADERSHIP EXPERIENCES

Our discussion on guided leadership experiences culminates in a carefully constructed series of learning experiences that lead to the aspiring leader growing in their self-efficacy. These leveled experiences will need to be navigated in a carefully constructed partnership to ensure the aspiring leader spends an appropriate amount of time developing before moving onto the next experience. We hope the provided examples help to illustrate the variety of ways you can create and foster guided leadership experiences for the aspiring leaders in your organization. In the next chapter, we will examine how we can ensure we are creating and celebrating mastery experiences, so that our aspiring leaders are ready to accept the challenges of becoming a principal.

SYSTEM CHECK

In seeking to better understand the importance of creating meaningful vicarious and guided learning experiences in an environment that fosters trust, consider the following questions:

1. Considering the local context of your organization, what might be priority experiences you would want your aspiring leader to engage first?

2. How is trust currently being modeled in your organization? Are teachers and leaders able to engage in collegial and collaborative observation of each other's practice?

IMPLEMENTATION POINTS TO PONDER

1. Consider asking your aspiring leaders what experiences they wish to have as they continue their professional learning. Make a list of the most noted requests, and how do these align with your local standards document or our ULS standards?

2. In thinking about the types of learning experiences you assistant principals have currently: Which area of the ULS do the learning experiences come under? Is there a greater focus on certain domains? What domains are currently being underserved?

3. Consider adding more professional learning on the topic of collegial trust to the professional development opportunities you offer to your assistant principals and principals. As the heart root, trust is key to effective mentorship!

PREDICTIVE INQUIRY

Use the following table to compare your predictions with the content presented in this chapter.

PLANNING GUIDED LEADERSHIP EXPERIENCES	
Predictions that were correct:	Questions I still have:
New information learned:	

ANSWER KEY TO ACTIVITY 4.1

Author Anonymous, A. Level 3; B. Level 2; C. Level 2; D. Level 3; E. Level 1; F. Level 2 or 3; G. Level 2; H. Level 1; I. Level 2; J. Level 2 or 3.

CHAPTER 5

ATTAINING MASTERY EXPERIENCES

Who has seen the wind? Neither you nor I. But when the trees bow down their heads, the wind is passing by.

—Christina Rossetti

FOUR ROOTS OF SCHOOL LEADER PREPARATION

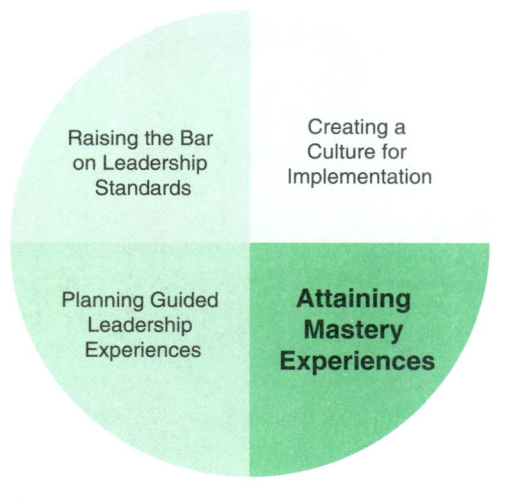

There are forces in nature that can uproot trees that have a shallow root system. Strong winds or excessive rain can also erode the soil, exposing roots, which can limit growth. But with the right conditions—a flexible trunk, thick bark, and temperate weather—the tree flourishes. In today's educational landscape, leaders are buffeted by similar forces. The pressure on principals is increasing and testing the strength of those in that role. The job is more complex than it once was, and a greater number of principals report poor work–life balance. Many also don't feel supported, and all these factors lead to higher attrition rates.

Yet as we've shown in these pages so far, we can be a force for good. We can guide assistant principals and principals through the challenges. Our final root is one that we think provides great sustenance to the "branches and foliage" of human development—for it involves the mentoring moves that help principal trainees flourish on their own.

 **UNIVERSAL LEADERSHIP STANDARDS FOCUS**

Growth and Innovation: This leadership standard reflects all capacities of continuous growth and systems excellence. This includes promoting opportunities for ongoing growth for all stakeholders. Leaders who focus on this standard create conditions for innovation and creativity through an environment that embraces risk-taking and experiential learning.

Learning and Engagement: This leadership standard reflects all capacities of instructional leadership. This may include decisions that directly impact the students, staff, and community stakeholders. Leaders who implement this standard acknowledge the impact of high-quality instruction on student learning and achievement.

WHAT MASTERY MEANS

Imagine walking along a pathway in a forest. You come to a clearing, which gives you a moment to look up and see the tallest trees against the sky. In the thick of the forest, you'd noticed their resilience, their massive trunks, surviving storms, and hundreds of seasons. Now you stand in awe of all the movement at the top, the upper branches bending and foliage seeming to dance in the wind. This is how we want you to envision the root of Attaining Mastery Experiences. We want our aspiring principals to reach a point of maturity where they are unwavering in their commitment to a shared vision and yet also humble and pliable as they approach mastery. We want those we train to see that mastery is not the end of growth, but the beginning of endless sky.

Mastery as a Beginning Not an End

Mastery is a word that we hear often in education. Mastery suggests a level of consistency in being able to reproduce a desired behavior or demonstrate a skill or technique. We speak often of helping students master the skills expected at each grade level. Proficiency, prowess, deftness, and expertise—all these terms are embedded in the concept of mastery. But perhaps because of the testing culture, educators often like to talk about mastery as a freeze frame, a pinnacle of excellence that you reach, and you are done. Well, we are here to say that's misguided. As author Alan B. Jones put it, "Masters are those who have simply started to see the difference in what they have learned and are yet to understand." One refines mastery forever. Our job is to

> *Proficiency, prowess, deftness, and expertise—all these terms are embedded in the concept of mastery.*

get more lead teachers, department heads, consultants, and coaches to step onto the pathway to assistant principalship and be "principal ready," at a level of mastery steady enough for the role.

ROOTED REFLECTION

Mastery can mean many different things to many different people. How would you define mastery in both an educational leadership context and a noneducational context? Do they differ? If so, why might that be?

Recapping the Journey Toward Mastery

We have covered a lot of ground thus far. We know that mastery does not happen overnight. As we have explored in this book, attaining mastery is a graduated process through which we systematically cultivate competency, confidence, and capacity. This is what it means to develop the self-efficacy of assistant principals. In Chapter 2, we talked about how universal leadership standards unite every individual in a school around a common cause. Our standards define *what we should be doing*. To help ensure assistant principals are well-versed in the various competencies that define their role, we recommended intentional, regular meetings.

In Chapter 3, we outlined six actions that help establish a culture of implementation for aspiring principals and across a school. The actions involve being present, observant, so as to know people—and know when they need our supportive feedback. In particular, we explored how to harness the will, skill, and thrill of each trainee, which helps us know *how we should be doing it*. How we should guide and motivate, based on the areas of growth the trainee identified as a priority. The reality is, when our assistant principals have real choice in their professional learning to address their needs, they feel valued and appreciated. They commit and perform better.

We know this from our research. For example, in the past, we were rather prescriptive with professional development (PD) topics and proceeded with a "you get what you get" attitude. This backfired. Our assistant principals expressed a wish to have more say. We obliged, aligning topics to their needs, thereby creating more targeted experiences. Many wanted to receive professional development in school operations early in the process; we were able to offer this too. The results were rewarding. Assistant principals reported higher levels of agency.

In Chapter 4, we made the case for providing trainees with guided leadership experiences that let strengths shine and less developed leadership muscles build. We explored ways to assure assistant principals gain a sense of what being a principal is really about. We shared how important it is to delegate, to increase rigor and challenge so the trainee is engaged.

Now, here in Chapter 5, we focus on four responsibilities involved in helping assistant principals who are on the cusp of attaining mastery.

1. Providing mastery experiences (increasing skill, will, and thrill)

2. Giving and receiving feedback

3. Knowing when mastery is achieved (expert noticing)

4. Celebrating the mastery experiences (realizing greater capacity)

Make no mistake—this is critical work at this stage, as assistant principals are most vulnerable to quitting. They are in deep enough that stress is high, and confidence can be low, so these four responsibilities are important to embrace. We will explore the why, when, and how of each one, but first, let's spend a moment looking at some key insights about mastery learning from research.

> *We focus on four responsibilities involved in helping assistant principals who are on the cusp of attaining mastery.*

WHAT THE RESEARCH SAYS ABOUT MASTERY EXPERIENCE

- Mastery experience is the most impactful aspect of Social Cognitive Learning theory in developing a higher sense of self-efficacy (Bandura, 1986, 1994; Negis-Isik & Derinbay, 2015).

- Mastery experience addresses the need for school leaders to have a level of competency with the essential knowledge and skills commensurate to those found in leadership standards (Australian Institute for Teaching and School Leadership, 2014; Dinham, Collarbone, Evans, & Mackay, 2013).

- Successful past experiences increase an individual's self-efficacy beliefs, whereas unsuccessful experiences have a negative impact on self-efficacy beliefs (Bandura, 2012).

- Leaders with higher levels of mastery are more prone to embrace change and confront challenges by leveraging high-yield strategies stemming from internally based personal power (Tschannen-Moran & Gareis, 2007).

- Efficacious leaders are those who can positively impact teaching and learning through establishing and fostering a sense of collective efficacy with teachers and staff (Louis, Leithwood, Wahlstrom, & Anderson, 2010).

Mastery experiences are generative—they help develop efficacious "master" leaders. As leaders we must both clear the way for these experiences to occur, and we must be able to determine when a trainee has achieved mastery. The four responsibilities ensure we do both these things.

ROOTED REFLECTION

In your current context (e.g., role, position, and assignment), what defines mastery? Who defines what mastery looks like? How do you know when you have reached mastery?

Providing Mastery Experiences
(Increasing Skill, Will, and Thrill)

One recurring theme in this book is the need to genuinely listen to and hear what assistant principals have to say in terms of the types of experiences they feel are needed to prepare them for further leadership roles. One thing we heard is this: they want relevant and rigorous experiences that align with the skills and competencies needed to become a principal. We owe it to them to deliver on this.

The word *relevance* is often accompanied by the word *rigor*. These qualities are both important to being a self-reflective practitioner. Relevance speaks to the reality that *what we learn* needs to be clear in terms of *why* we are learning it. For example, when our division made a shift in assessment practice from percentages to levels of achievement, our assistant principals needed to understand the rationale behind this central decision so that they could best support teachers in the changes to teacher gradebooks. So as a division, we set our focus on ongoing outcomes-based assessment and reporting. Knowing the massive shift in grading practices that we were embarking on over the next five years, we deliberately set the focus of year one to gaining confidence and efficacy in the understanding and application of these practices. To do so, we needed to bring in our in-house assessment experts. Working with assessment consultants, we planned ample Level 2 professional learning experiences for the assistant principals. These experiences included learning the new gradebook, understanding how differentiation for inclusive needs was to be achieved, and anticipating the time needed to provide elbow support for teachers learning the new gradebooks.

Rigor speaks to *how we learn*. When we strive for rigor in the learning experiences we design, we are talking about those sweet spots of complexity and challenge where growth and engagement happens. In light of the gradual release of the responsibility model (Pearson & Gallagher, 1983), the sweet spot is the learner's zone of proximal development (ZDP). Put plainly, the ZDP is a task that makes the learner sweat but doesn't challenge to the point of frustration or overwhelm. We know this research well in the context of teaching students, but trust us, the mentor/protégé dynamic is just as important. With adults, the key is to authentically involve them as partners rather than subordinates. For example, when our assistant principals were included in the planning and process work for making the shift to our new reporting methodology, they demonstrated more commitment (not buy-in) to the process. Why? They felt that they were part of the collective work and through this held a greater degree of responsibility for the success moving forward. Mastery experiences don't occur without high levels of responsibility.

> *When we strive for rigor in the learning experiences we design, we are talking about those sweet spots of complexity and challenge.*

As we have said, moving aspiring leaders from Level 2 experiences (guided learning) toward Level 3 experiences (mastery) can take time depending on the skill or competency to be learned. Knowing when to prompt, push, or pull the protégé out of their comfort zone is central to being an effective mentor. If things are too easy, overconfidence or disengagement with the significance of the learning can manifest. Too hard and the learner can be quickly discouraged or disinclined to press into the learning at hand.

Plan for Disequilibrium

You must anticipate—and plan for—these moments of trainee disequilibrium. For example, when we shifted to outcomes-based assessment and reporting, we built into our professional learning plan time for additional learning sessions. We knew there would be those who wanted more support or needed a little more time to get to Level 3. Assistant principals who attained Level 3 earlier on were invited to connect with another colleague and help support their learning. Throughout the process of our shift in practice, we noted lower instances of stress and anxiety. So, it is really a matter of how we move assistant principals from Level 2 to Level 3 with appropriate levels of relevance and rigor that breed success. The design of professional learning cannot be left to chance.

> *Knowing when to prompt, push, or pull the protégé out of their comfort zone is central to being an effective mentor.*

Following are some recommendations we give protégés that can help them be immersed in relevant and rigorous learning routines that move them toward mastery. Recall that **skill** speaks to what prior knowledge the aspiring leader brings with them; **will** refers to the aspiring leader and their disposition toward leading; and **thrill** seeks to understand the leader's motivations (Figure 5.1).

FIGURE 5.1 FIVE WAYS TO ENGAGE DURING RELEVANT AND
RIGOROUS ROUTINES

RECOMMENDATION	SKILL	WILL	THRILL
Root practice in leadership standards with well-defined and specific goals	✔		
Give each part of your goals/subgoals your full attention	✔	✔	
Be comfortable being uncomfortable: move out of your comfort zone		✔	✔
Maintain your motivation by celebrating successes			✔
Get feedback from a master	✔	✔	✔

Notice that the skill, will, and thrill boxes each have three check marks; this helps us appreciate that the five recommendations indeed fuel different aspects of a trainee's capacity. Now look at the last row, and notice that feedback spans across, ringing the chimes of the skill, will, and thrill. Feedback is paramount to the success of any routine and essential to the development of mastery in our aspiring leaders. We know that Level 2 Experiences require a greater level or frequency of feedback, whereas at Level 3, we would expect feedback only as required or to recalibrate a particular competency.

We will explore giving and receiving feedback in more depth in the next section, but because it's such a critical part of planning and guiding mastery experiences, we want to share some essential types of it now.

The Center for Creative Leadership outlines the four types of feedback that are most effective when communicating in a peer-to-peer or mentor-to-mentee relationship. See the following section for their definitions of feedback.

THE MOST EFFECTIVE TYPES OF FEEDBACK

1. **Directive** feedback tells someone what to do, even if you're phrasing it "nicely." For example, "*I suggest that you make priorities clearer to your team.*"

2. **Contingency** feedback gives a future consequence: "*If you keep interrupting people in meetings, they'll stop cooperating with you.*"

3. **Attribution** feedback describes someone or their actions in terms of a quality or label, as in "*You're a good communicator*" or "*You're undisciplined.*"

4. **Impact** feedback, on the other hand, informs the receiver about the effect their actions have had on other people or on the organization. Impact feedback is important in performance reviews because it can shed light on something your direct report never knew or thought about. It gets at "why" their behaviors are either working or not working. An example of impact feedback is: "*Team members were confused, and I felt frustrated.*"

Source: Adapted from Center for Creative Leadership (2020).

Knowing these types of feedback helps us as leaders be more intentional as we coach trainees. Now let's turn to the nuances of using it well.

Giving and Receiving Feedback (Expert Noticing)

Leaders who are masters at providing feedback generally have parameters when it comes to the language they choose to apply. It is important to understand that it isn't simply what you choose to say, but how you deliver the feedback to an aspiring leader. Here are some common things to avoid when engaging in the feedback process:

1. The feedback judges individuals, not actions.

2. The feedback is too vague.

3. The feedback speaks for others.

4. Negative feedback gets sandwiched between positive messages.

5. The feedback is exaggerated with generalities.

6. The feedback psychoanalyzes the motives behind behavior.

7. The feedback goes on too long.

8. The feedback contains an implied threat.

9. The feedback uses inappropriate humor.

10. The feedback is a question, not a statement.

Source: Adapted from Center for Creative Leadership (2020).

As our leaders move through our leveled experiences, it is important for us to determine when they may be ready to undertake a new challenge. They will be ready when they exhibit elements of mastery. Ensuring our leaders are demonstrating mastery requires us to lean on our own personal expertise to seek out indications of success. This is demonstrated in our classrooms by teachers who use "teacher expert noticing." When our teachers have a rich understanding of their students, and the standards the students are working toward, they can engage in an active process of interpretation of what they see in the learner. From this point, expert teachers determine the next course of action for their students. In order for teachers to yield this expertise, teachers must:

1. draw on their own content knowledge within the domain of new learning;

2. see the new learning from the perspective of the learner;

3. recognize how the learner may approach the new content.

This is no different than what is required of leaders as they seek to identify mastery in aspiring school leaders. There needs to be elements of *expert leadership noticing* that are developed to ensure we are prepared to evaluate mastery. When we leaders engage in the active process of attending to what is happening in a particular experience and then interpret what they see according to the desired outcomes, we can be more deliberate in the preparation of our leaders.

Engage in Expert Noticing

Engaging in expert noticing requires us to:

1. Be selective and upfront about what we are seeking to identify.

2. Inform our aspiring leader about the shared expectations for experiential learning.

3. Refine what we seek to notice to ensure we are developing a specific competency.

4. Look for successes as well as areas of improvement with our aspiring leader.

Here is an example of these four phases of expert noticing in action. In being *selective and upfront* with her assistant principal, Principal Gertie Heinz is deliberate in her communication about what she is looking for. "When I seek to observe my leaders, I remember to tell them not to sweat the big stuff. In fact, we highlight small observable actions that both they and I feel need to be developed." By identifying the smaller actions taken by aspiring leaders (*shared expectations for experiential learning*), we become more aware of what we are unable to do. For example, at the beginning of the school year, Gertie has her assistant principal at the front of the school greeting new students and their parents. "From this point, I am looking at how my leaders are welcoming parents into our school environment and ensuring they are warm, inviting, and respectful." This highlights the significance of community and culture at Riverview Elementary. When it comes to *refining and developing a specific competency*, Gertie stated: "In thinking about the many tasks I assign my assistant principal, it is important that specific feedback is provided in as timely fashion as possible through multiple means." Gertie and her assistant principal met prior to this observation to discuss what means of communication and feedback are most effective in this case. "My leadership team enjoys face-to-face meetings post-observation as they can engage in a reflective conversation, and we can chat about what I noticed versus what they perceived." In this case, Gertie engaged in a pre-meeting to set the expectations of the observation, and a post-meeting where both parties could have an open discussion about the experience. These actions speak to the importance of looking for successes as well as additional areas for growth.

Finding what works best for you and your team will require you to engage in these preconversations with your aspiring leaders to determine the type, frequency, and intensity of observations. Most importantly, your role and responsibility will be to notice areas of strength and areas for growth. Here are a few questions that can be used as we seek to notice mastery with our aspiring leaders.

REFLECTION QUESTIONS FOR EXPERT NOTICING

1. What am I noticing about the aspiring leader as they engage in leadership tasks?

2. What does their engagement tell me about their current dispositions, unique characteristics, and leadership opportunities?

3. How does my observation differ from the aspiring leader's reflection on the experience?

Source: Adapted from Sherin, Jacobs, & Philipp (2011).

Using the above questions (while maintaining the perspective of the aspiring leader) will afford us the opportunity to be evaluative without being judgmental as we seek to build mastery experiences. Naturally it should be noted that exercising a feedback loop will be paramount to ensuring our aspiring leaders continue to feel supported as they realize greater capacity for leadership.

A Cautionary Tale for Expert Noticing

How does a mentor know if their protégé is overconfident? This is an important aspect of mentoring and coaching because overconfidence can lead to potentially negative outcomes or allow bad habits to take root. It can enable a protégé to take shortcuts or lower their guard in terms of follow-through on best practices. This could have unintended consequences. Typically, this comes in the form of not adjusting a course of action or heeding contrary advice in favor of a fixed mindset of "this is how we always do things." Further, we know from research on adult learning (andragogy) that "Individuals who are highly assured in their capabilities and the effectiveness of their strategies are disinclined to seek discordant information that would suggest the need for corrective adjustments (Bandura, 2009, p. 181). This is why knowing the affective state and how to ask great meditative questions is so helpful. This is also where checklists, mental maps, rehearsal, and exemplars are great additions to a rigorous development regimen. Consider airline pilots or naval navigators who go through a prescribed set of checks and balances. These routine checks are done regardless of their level of mastery. The checks are performed to ensure fidelity to the conceptual and practical aspects required to perform the task of flying the plane or sailing the ship. Mentors must not take for granted that just because an aspiring leader says or feels that they have the concept mastered, that they actually do. This is not meant to suggest that we should doubt or second guess, rather, as a mentor, we must truly be able to affirm that the protégé is at the presumed level of capability. Again, this is why knowing your people and meeting them where they are at is so key.

Another consideration that we feel is very important for central leaders/ mentors to be mindful of is the need to bracket potential personal bias in terms of our own personal leadership development/formation experiences. How we cut our leadership teeth back in the day versus the many nuances that exist in a multigenerational workforce today are markedly different. What is deemed important to a particular generation of leaders might not necessarily apply to a newer generation. For example, a Generation X principal (Tim) may feel that a person's years of experience and commitment to the profession are more important to advancement than a range of outside experiences an aspiring leader from Generation Y or a Millennial (Vince) may have. Whereas an aspiring leader from Generation Y is less inclined to be a "company person" and sees advancement based on ability, capability, and desire versus needing to have a set number of years of experience. Thus, it remains important for mentors to be in tune with the worldviews that exist today versus how it was "back in the good old days." Moreover, it is important that aspiring leaders have realistic expectations of the process and commensurate level of mastery needed to advance to principalship. This is one of the important and cautionary functions the mentor must fulfill. We will next look at some ways to help determine mastery.

Capacity Realization (Not Just Capacity Building)

We often hear a lot about capacity building. We want to provide aspiring leaders with more than a threshold of the competencies they are to know, understand, and be able to perform. We want them to be able to take on new challenges with success. But capacity building, we argue, does not hit the mark for what is really needed. What we need is to shift our focus from capacity building to capacity realization. What do we mean by this? Imagine that you have just charged your smartphone to 100%. Your device is at full capacity. It cannot hold any more energy. In essence, it is at full capacity. Now imagine that you simply leave the phone on your desk for a few days without using it. Separation anxiety aside, if you have full capacity but do not use that capacity or leverage it in any way, what benefit or impact are you realizing? The answer is none. Thus, it is one thing to develop capacity. But to affect change, to see tangible action, we need to *realize* capacity. We need to create conditions that put the potential energy to work so to speak.

Knowing When Mastery Is Achieved (Realizing Greater Capacity)

How many road trips have you been on when someone asks, "are we there yet?" While we know that it's the journey that matters most, we need more aspiring leaders to reach the destination of the pathway! Realizing more assistant principals joining the ranks of principals is the sunny destination we are seeking. Knowing when our aspiring leaders are ready to step onto the path is what leaders and mentors must be able to discern.

Recall that we define a Level 1 experiences as a surface level of knowledge and understanding on a given concept. We can read, observe, and listen all we want about a topic and achieve a very high level of knowledge about it, and like the phone, be at 100% capacity of "the what." But unless we are doing something with what we have learned (the premise of Level 2 experiences), we are not realizing any tangible benefit other than perhaps being "book smart." To move from guided learning to mastery learning requires moving beyond intention. It requires connecting potential directly to implementation. Realizing capacity means providing our assistant principals relevant and rigorous practical learning experiences. Recall in Chapter 1 where we discussed the move from potential to implementation using Figure 1.3 (Figure 5.2 here; please look at the accompanying Figure 5.3 as a parallel comparison.

Being deliberate in our capacity building will yield the capacity realization necessary for mastery.

FIGURE 5.2   MOVING FROM POTENTIAL TO IMPLEMENTATION

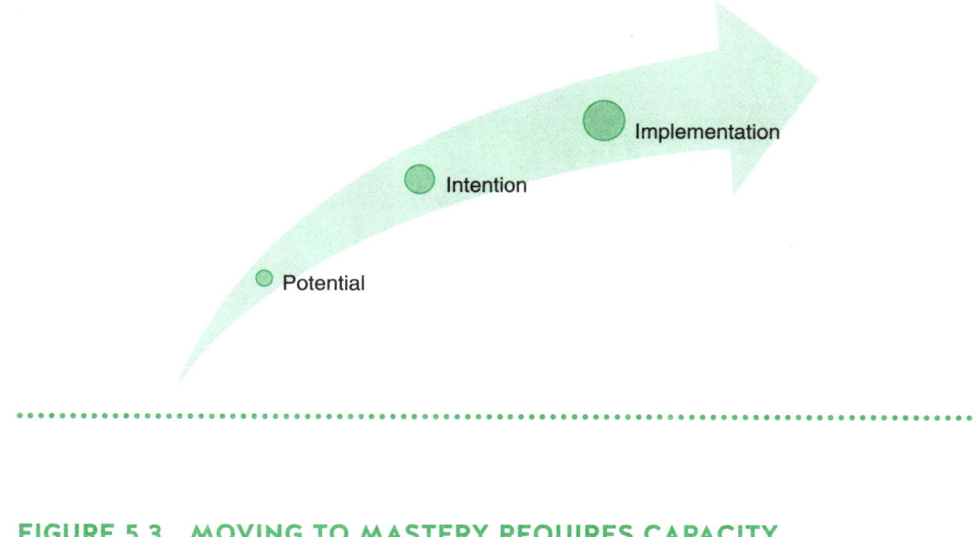

FIGURE 5.3   MOVING TO MASTERY REQUIRES CAPACITY REALIZATION

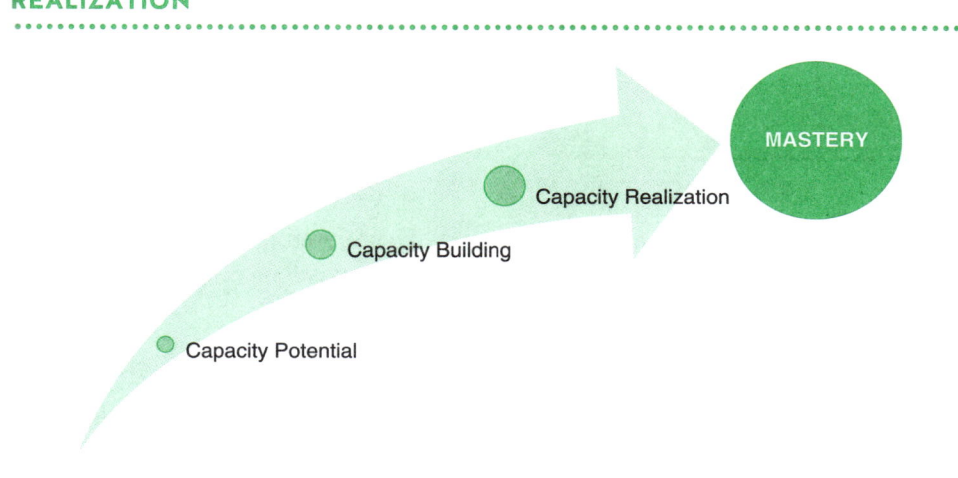

WHAT DOES MASTERY AT LEVEL 3 LOOK LIKE?

As an assistant principal moves from gaining a surface level of knowledge and understanding about a given topic (Level 1) to a more hands-on practical application of skills with guided support (Level 2), we know that the desired state is to reach Level 3 (mastery). This is easily said. But what does this look like? How do we move from guided learning to mastery learning? To answer this, it is important to remember that the skills and competencies in question stem from our leadership standards.

Let's recall the four leadership standards we proposed in Chapter 2. A synthesis of many sets of standards from around the globe, these are the building blocks upon which leadership skills and competencies are predicated. For your convenience we have added the standards once more.

Stewardship of Stakeholder Learning and Engagement: This leadership standard reflects all capacities of instructional leadership. This may include decisions that directly impact the students, staff, and community stakeholders. Leaders who implement this standard acknowledge the impact of high-quality instruction on student learning and achievement.

Stewardship of Resources and Operations: This leadership standard reflects all capacities of managerial and adherence to state regulations or legislation. This may include decisions involving the deployment of finances, human capital, materials, and infrastructure to best support the learning community.

Stewardship of Community and Culture: This leadership standard reflects all capacities of moral and ethical leadership. This may include the fostering of collegial and communal trust, inclusive and caring communities. Leaders who focus on this standard consciously create supportive environments to best serve all students in their community.

Stewardship of Growth and Innovation: This leadership standard reflects all capacities of continuous growth and systems excellence. This includes promoting opportunities for ongoing growth for all stakeholders. Leaders who focus on this standard create conditions for innovation and creativity through an environment that embraces risk-taking and experiential learning.

As a means of illustration of what moving from Level 2 to Level 3 looks like, let's look at a few examples of common tasks often assigned to assistant principals and break down the game film on the nuances between moving from guided learning to mastery learning. Keep in mind that these are only some of the examples of how our aspiring leaders can move through mastery of each level. We have left some space after each example for you to jot down some ideas, reflections, or thoughts that arise. One way to utilize these spaces could be to include how you see this working in your local context.

Examples of Level 2 to Level 3 Experiences (Figures 5.4–5.7)

FIGURE 5.4   ULS 1: LEARNING AND ENGAGEMENT LEVELED TASKS

STANDARD	TASK/SUBSKILLS	LEVEL 2 (HIGH LEVEL OF MENTOR GUIDANCE)	LEVEL 3 (NOMINAL TO NO GUIDANCE REQUIRED)
Learning and Engagement	Instructional supervision (classroom observation, debriefing with teachers, preparing evaluation documentation, and providing feedback)	– Accompanies principal on a few observations, debriefs following observations, and then is assigned to do some observations on their own. – Uses exemplars of prepost lesson discussion questions (including mediative questions). – Has written feedback vetted by principal for summative documents. – Contributes to the final assessment document. Is conversant with teacher quality standards. – May oversee a full process for one or two teachers.	– Has autonomy to schedule classroom visits with teachers. – Can competently conduct prepost lesson debriefings. – Is adept at offering pedagogical and assessment advice to increase instructional praxis. Fluent with teacher quality standards. – Provides timely feedback to principal with recommendations for next steps – Can conduct a full assessment process for any teachers requiring evaluation.

Key Ideas or Reflections From Above:

FIGURE 5.5 ULS 2: RESOURCES AND OPERATIONS LEVELED TASKS

STANDARD	TASK/SUBSKILLS	LEVEL 2 (HIGH LEVEL OF MENTOR GUIDANCE)	LEVEL 3 (NOMINAL TO NO GUIDANCE REQUIRED)
Resources and Operations	Field trips (coordinating local, state, national, and international trips pursuant to expectations in policy and legal frameworks)	– Knows expectations and corresponding logistics/policy for conducting various field trips. – Learns procedure for vetting volunteers and having appropriate supervision ratios. – Can complete forms and for principal review/signature. – Has multiple opportunities to support planning of local/state trips.	– Can capably assist teachers and staff with process and ensure fidelity to admin procedure/policy. – Can liaise confidently with divisional leadership/other agencies regarding travel insurance/cancellation, medical, etc., for more complicated trips, for example, international travel. – Can capably oversee field trips as part of admin portfolio.

Key Ideas or Reflections From Above:

FIGURE 5.6 ULS 3: COMMUNITY AND CULTURE LEVELED TASKS

STANDARD	TASK/SUBSKILLS	LEVEL 2 (HIGH LEVEL OF MENTOR GUIDANCE)	LEVEL 3 (NOMINAL TO NO GUIDANCE REQUIRED)
Community and Culture	Breakfast/lunch programs (liaising with community/other agency partnerships, volunteer pool, and general program logistics)	– Understands the wider societal needs in the community. – Can articulate the logistics required to support the program: funding, staffing, equipment, and accountability needs. – Participates in hiring/support of corresponding staff. – Is conversant with government regulations and reporting requirements.	– Advocates for and champions programs within local/wider community. – Can lead school through inspections/ program reviews with other agencies. – Can capably provide program data and produce corresponding school-level reports for stakeholders. – Can confidently lead this program as part of wider portfolio.

Note: This would be similar for specialty programs as well such as International Baccalaureate, Advanced Placement, Athletic Academies, STEM, etc.

Key Ideas or Reflections From Above:

FIGURE 5.7 ULS 4: GROWTH AND INNOVATION LEVELED TASKS

STANDARD	TASK/SUBSKILLS	LEVEL 2 (HIGH LEVEL OF MENTOR GUIDANCE)	LEVEL 3 (NOMINAL TO NO GUIDANCE REQUIRED)
Growth and Innovation	High school completion (working with other stakeholders to ensure that high school students are meeting eligibility for state requirements, mentoring students, and programming needs)	– Can access and interpret local data to understand general areas of need. – Works with school stakeholders, for example, students, teachers, counselors, coaches, parents to articulate pathways and programming needs. – Works with other agencies/ departments to understand and access broader supports that are available.	– Can speak to trends in data and advocate for needs arising from the data. – Coordinates efforts of a wider team to ensure every student is on pace/knows what supports are needed. – Finds creative solutions/ alternative means for students to get courses needed for credentialing.

Key Ideas or Reflections From Above:

FIGURE 5.8   THINGS TO LOOK FOR IN DETERMINING MASTERY

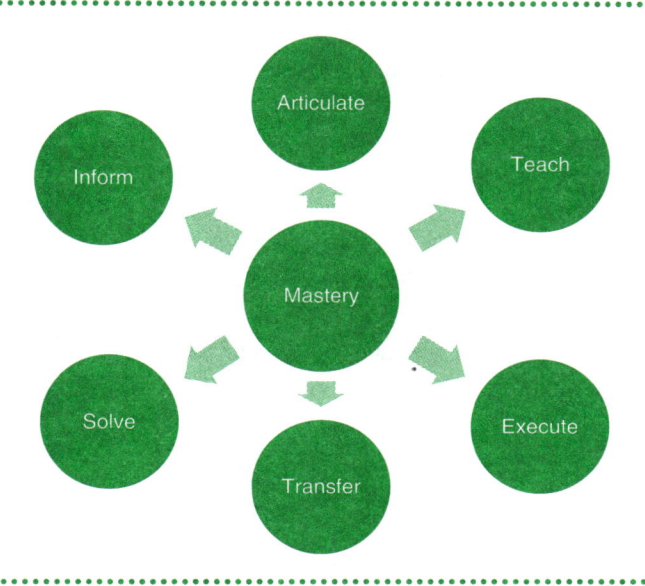

Here is a list of a few actions that you can notice in yourself (as an aspiring leader) or in others (if you are in a mentorship type role).

- You can **articulate** robust understanding of the concept criteria and **teach** it to others.
- You can consistently **execute** tasks effectively and efficiently (without mentor support).
- You can **adapt** and **transfer** concepts to new/different contexts.
- You can **solve** unique challenges and innovate new ways of doing things.
- You remain committed to informing your practice through lifelong learning.

Of course, these are not exhaustive examples; however, we do suggest keeping these action words handy as you are gaining mastery in your leadership role.

LISTENING TO THE VOICES OF ASSISTANT PRINCIPALS

Pat (K–9) "My current principal has told me that I possess those skills needed to be a principal of a school. I have learned a great deal from the principal that I work with and feel that in the future my path will lead me to pursue becoming principal of a school."

Tyrone (Junior High) "When I became an assistant principal, I felt that I did not aspire to principalship. Why? In my first year as AP, my principal told me I would likely not go far as an administrator. While I wanted to quit, another principal told me to stick with it. I did. Having since served in the role now for a number of years, with two very different principals, I have changed my mind and now believe that I have the skill set and education that would support me in becoming a principal."

Val (High School) "I have had the opportunity to work for excellent principals who have given me the opportunity to build my own leadership capacity. Although I know the learning curve will be steep and I won't fully understand all of the demands until I am in that role, I feel I have a solid foundation and am willing and able to take on this challenge."

ROOTED REFLECTION

- When you think of mentorship, what comes to mind in terms of *the role and responsibility of the principal* when you read Pat and Tyrone's comments?

- To what extent do you agree or disagree with Val's comment about principalship: "I won't fully understand all of the demands until I am in that role." Discuss with a colleague.

LISTENING TO THE VOICE OF
WAYNE DAVIES

Vice Principal: Nelson McIntyre Collegiate Institute—Winnipeg Manitoba, Canada

A few years into my journey as a principal, I was paired with a brand-new vice principal. Alex was smart, hardworking, and loved students. Early on, we began having conversations about what we both wanted for the school, the students, the staff, and ourselves. We agreed on many things including engaging the community, especially the families of our students. It was definitely an area Alex was passionate about.

We also agreed on something else. We had seen vice principals "side lined" in other schools. Alex was too talented and promising a future principal to waste stagnating on menial tasks. Thus, I set a target of helping Alex build efficacy in this as well as several other dimensions. My goal was to expose Alex to a variety of ideas and skills and then provide support incorporating those into practice, able to apply them to situations not yet encountered.

Throughout that first semester, we faced many challenges but none so devastating to student and staff morale as a critical incident that drew extremely negative national media attention. Parents' and students' confidence in the school was shaken and we needed to respond. We worked with the students and staff to create a whole-school exhibition of skills and talents for the elementaries that provided students to us. They and their parents needed to be reassured that our school was a safe and engaging place. The bulk of the organizing was done by me and students with Alex taking on smaller aspects of the event. Alex also picked up the slack while I was occupied with preparations. Once we got to "game day," Alex was a huge help, jumping in where necessary to smooth issues and provide assistance to others.

Shortly thereafter Alex and I began talking about doing another event that might continue to reestablish our school as a positive member of the greater community. I asked Alex to come up with an idea or two. Shortly thereafter Alex requested a meeting with a community member known for their leadership in philanthropic work. After the meeting, Alex presented me with a proposal for a community sports equipment "swap meet." Community members could bring in gently used equipment that other community members could then take home to use with their families. It would answer a real need as many of our families were under economic pressures, yet still wanted their children to lead active lifestyles.

I quickly realized that Alex had been watching closely during the school exposition and was ready to apply those lessons. After a bit more tweaking and talking, I asked Alex to lead the event. I stayed close, but out of the way enough for Alex to make decisions and demonstrate readiness to move from participant to leader, occasionally asking questions or nudging Alex to look where things might have been missed. Alex led our students and several community and staff volunteers in putting on a needed and well-received event, complete with some very positive media attention for the school and community.

CELEBRATING MASTERY

We all enjoy a good party! Throughout life there are many milestones that we celebrate. When our assistant principals achieve mastery in any of the wide array of skills and competencies inherent to their role, to what extent do we celebrate their accomplishments? While there may be some form of formal recognition, for example, permanent designation or continuous status in the role, when an assistant principal meets the expectations set by their school jurisdiction for tenure, we are most interested in recognizing and celebrating the little steps along the way. Each step after all leads to the next, and a little recognition and encouragement goes a long way to keeping a spring in our step!

When we build a stronger sense of efficacy in the small things, we believe it transcends to the larger tasks and responsibilities that come with the role. Bandura (2009) reminds us that "a resilient sense of efficacy provides the necessary staying power in the tortuous pursuit of innovation and excellence"

> *Creating a culture that does not dwell upon setbacks but rather affirms learner success is the key.*

(p. 183). Let's face it, we need our assistant principals to stay. If we lose them to burnout or other forms of attrition, then we do not realize the next generation of principals that we so urgently need. Author Michael Fullan (2018) reminds us that the role of principal has changed fundamentally in the past few years. The nuances of complexity and challenge in our ever-changing world call us, as system and school leaders, to realize deeper levels of collaboration, determination, and accountability for the cultural conditions within our own leadership formation programs. Creating a culture that does not dwell upon setbacks but rather affirms learner success is the key. Though honoring their essential role and the vital work of our assistant principals, we can let them know that they are valued and appreciated. Furthermore, we can impress upon them that we need them. We need them to take that next step…with confidence!

WAYS TO CELEBRATE MASTERY MILESTONES

We know that taking the time to honor and celebrate small steps goes a long way to team building and retention. Here are a few low (or no) cost ways to affirm the victories and successes of your assistant principals.

- Leverage the power of gratitude through genuine expressions of appreciation and thanks.

- Take time to thank individuals—in person is best, but a call, email, text, or card works too!

- Consider a formal acknowledgment at a school board meeting that recognizes aspiring leaders when they make progress in key competencies, for example, when they complete a professional learning course or microcredential.

- Share milestone and praise-worthy successes in a division newsletter or website.

- Provide a small keepsake that reminds them of the skill, will, and thrill of your leadership formation programming.

- Gift them with a book or other professional learning resource that marks their progress.

- Give shout-outs (bouquets) at leadership meetings/PD events.

Celebrating mastery is a powerful part of mentorship. We absolutely want assistant principals to achieve a Level 3 suite of skills and competencies. But what comes next can be challenging for the mentor. We must not trivialize success nor water it down, instead we need to put on our social persuasion caps once more and encourage our Level 3 aspiring leaders to "leave the nest" and get on the pathway to principalship. Let's examine this in more detail.

MOVING THE LEVEL 3 ASSISTANT PRINCIPAL ONTO THE PATHWAY

When assistant principals grow in self-efficacy and can perform a suite of expected tasks consistently with little to no supervision, they are at a level of functioning that we would arguably call "Level 3" (mastery). In the spirit of lifelong learning and leading, we acknowledge that there is always more to learn and that we cannot rest on our laurels. Improvement is always possible! By realizing greater capacity in the day-to-day tasks of assistant principalship, aspiring principals can gain greater insight into the required managerial and operational tasks, but more so, will be better prepared to face the "fundamental dilemmas in administration" (Marshall, 1993, p. 89). In Chapter 1, we spoke of the increasing challenge and complexity of the role of principalship. Because an assistant principal presents with a high degree of readiness (Level 3 skillset), we cannot take for granted that they will pursue the next step on the pathway. This is why we want to come back briefly to talk once more about social persuasion.

It is often difficult to convince someone to leave an existing environment where they may feel content and comfortable, especially if they are a solid contributor to a successful school culture. When you have assistant principals who are ready to leave the nest, sometimes as a principal or systems leader, you need to provide that gentle nudge or push. Recall, our premise for realizing leadership capacity insists that we do something with (actively use) the Level 3 skills that have been developed. We need more principals, urgently. So, once we have achieved getting more assistant principals to Level 3 skills, we need to have earnest conversations about taking that next step onto the pathway to principalship.

Think back to our three key words from Chapter 3: **calming, cautioning,** and **counseling**. As system leaders and mentors, we must encourage Level 3 assistant principals to understand that they are needed now more than ever to step into the next role. Reassuring them of divisional or jurisdictional support for moving into principalship is a critical step. Affirming the skill, will, and thrill of principalship in relation to your perceptions and validation of them as a Level 3 leader can go a long way to getting them onto the path. As always, there is need for caution and counseling. While attaining Level 3 skills is the key for realizing greater self-efficacy, it is not possible to fully prepare an assistant principal to be a principal until they are sitting in the chair! Remember, we want them to take that next step onto the pathway. Reassuring them that a divisional support system including further mentorship and development will be in place is integral to them taking that next step. They want to know that they have a true champion walking alongside them. This is important because we know that the move from assistant principal to principal means a shift in professional identity. Helping new principals adjust to this identity change is important and we know that a similar levels of experience approach akin to what we want to do for assistant principals would be helpful (but that is a topic for another book).

ACTIVITY 5.1 MOVING A RELUCTANT LEADER FORWARD

Meet Corey. Now in her fifth year as assistant principal at Northern Bear Regional High. Corey lives and breathes this school. She attended it as a student, served as a teacher, was Physical Education Department head, and is now serving as assistant principal with Grade 12 coordinator, athletics, social studies, academic scheduling, and commencement coordinator as part of the broader portfolio. You are Corey's principal. You are confident that Corey is predominantly at a Level 3 skillset. Corey does not require much (if any) direction, is proactive, a good communicator, and takes initiative when needed. Knowing that your school division is in need of more principals, you express your belief that you feel Corey is ready to move forward and casually inquire about future plans. Here is what Corey tells you:

> I don't feel confident yet that I can take on the role and responsibilities of the principal. There has been ample opportunity for professional development for leaders in our district, but I still feel that I have had limited experiences. I've also watched you over the past couple of years and know how challenging things get and all the demands on your time. Plus, I love this school. Why would I want to leave? Once a Bear. . .always a Bear!

1. What further questions does this raise for you as Corey's principal/ mentor?

2. What do you feel is the next best step to encourage Corey to move forward?

3. How would you respond to Corey? With a colleague, take a turn role playing as the principal and then as Corey. Think about affective state, social persuasion, trust, and the levels of experience as you role play. Focus on using meditative questions akin to those in Chapter 3.

In what ways do you recognize and celebrate mastery learning exhibited by your aspiring leaders?

IMPLEMENTATION POINTS TO PONDER

1. Which root or roots: Leadership Standards, Culture of Implementation, Guided Leadership Experiences, and Mastery Experiences might serve as your next area of focus for professional development of your assistant principals?

2. One of the greatest calls to action from the research over the past 50 years is to provide more practical experiences for assistant principals. This means creating more mastery learning opportunities versus talking about the need to do more. How might you make an intentional shift away from *capacity building* in favor of implementing a greater measure of *capacity realization*? What would this look like for your jurisdiction?

PREDICTIVE INQUIRY

Use the following table to compare your predictions with the content presented in this chapter.

ATTAINING MASTERY EXPERIENCES	
Predictions that were correct:	Questions I still have:
New information learned:	

CONCLUSION

Implementing the Four Roots—Our Perspectives

E arlier in the book we shared that only about one-third of participants in my (Tim) study indicated a desire to pursue principalship. The data were collected in September 2019, which, notably, was prepandemic. That is, before the additional stressors of trying to sustain schools in remote and hybrid models. When we conducted a follow-up in April of 2022 (with essentially the same population of assistant principals), we were heartened to discover a noticeable increase in the number of individuals wanting to become a principal. Despite the challenges and struggles inherent to the global pandemic, despite the realization that the role of principal remains complex and challenging, we observed a 10% increase in the number of potential principals. This is a HUGE increase in such a short period of time, something that we definitely celebrated!

> *Despite the challenges and struggles inherent to the global pandemic, despite the realization that the role of principal remains complex and challenging, we observed a 10% increase in the number of potential principals.*

For this school division this equates to 10% more aspiring leaders wanting to journey along the pathway to principalship! The increase offers both reassurance and hope that more assistant principals will brave the walk along the pathway as they are rooted in practices to grow their leadership capacity. In wanting to understand what might help explain the shift, we asked assistant principals to offer commentary on what they felt was a game changer. Here are some of the top reasons they provided:

1. We feel more valued and appreciated because we have been included in more professional development activities that mirror what our principals are doing.

2. We have had multiple opportunities to share our ideas in terms of the types of experiences we need and feel that our voices have been heard.

3. Principals are being asked to be more consistent across the division in terms of mentoring and providing learning experiences for us.

4. We have been included in more practical operational learning experiences at the division level including school budgeting, resource management, instructional planning and supervision, as well as school visioning and growth planning.

5. We are included in a wider array of central communications and have people in the central office who champion our professional growth and learning.

So, now that we have had time to implement more practical experiences for our assistant principals, we invited them to share their perspectives:

> *The increase in those wanting to become a principal offers both reassurance and hope that we can not only stem the tide of principal attrition but turn it in favor of having deeper pools of talent to draw upon.*

With the knowledge that more must be done to support our assistant principals, our jurisdiction has commenced implementation of the roots. Although disrupted by the COVID-19 pandemic and still in its early stages, we are beginning to realize more assistant principals embracing the roots of leadership and are already seeing more aspiring principals step onto the pathway. Furthermore, when canvassed two years later (January 2022), the cadre of assistant principals in our jurisdiction (predominately the same group as in Cusack, 2020) demonstrated an increase in the desire to serve as a principal (see Figure 6.1). Here is what a few of them had to say:

LISTENING TO THE VOICES OF ASSISTANT PRINCIPALS

Alice (Elementary) "I am grateful for the many opportunities to learn skills that will help us with the many hats we wear as APs. The more knowledge and experience in this role, the more prepared and confident we can be to reach the next step of principalship or other roles of servant leaders within the Division. The role of AP is indeed unique and gratifying, and it is great to be able to have support to realize further capacity. Thank you for the opportunity to share our thoughts and PD wish lists!"

Carlos (Junior High) "Mentorship of APs has been very beneficial; to network and learn a variety of responsibilities. I'm interested in inter-visitations at other school sites. Getting perspective of other school cultures, responsibilities allocated to other APs, gain new ideas and initiatives implemented at the school. I think a lot of APs get stressed about things we have little exposure to such as budget, time calculators, etc. There has been more of an effort to include us this year. Thank you!"

Suria (K–9) "I truly appreciate your support and effort in the past few years to ensure that APs are heard and valued in their designated role. You have been our number one supporter and have provided opportunities to learn and grow. I love being included and invited to some of the principal meetings, as it provides us with firsthand knowledge and information of the division's updates. Any meeting that we can be involved in is beneficial to our role of supporting the principal. I value and respect all that you continue to do for the AP group and the division as a whole."

FIGURE 6.1   ASSISTANT PRINCIPALS WERE ASKED IF THEY WANTED TO BECOME A PRINCIPAL

YEAR	YES	NO	UNCERTAIN
2019	35 (%)	21 (%)	44 (%)
2022	45 (%)	17 (%)	38 (%)

ROOTED REFLECTION

1. What stands out for you in reading the testimonials above?

2. What aspects of guided to mastery learning experiences do you notice in any of the three testimonials.

3. What insights do these three assistant principals offer you at systems leadership level?

What are some other areas for growth or support to consider based upon feedback from our assistant principals? Here is what they suggested:

- Offer sessions specifically tailored to women in leadership with a mentor principal who could speak to the challenges and successes of women in the role.

- Establish a manual or a guide of specific duties month by month. This might provide a better idea of what is strictly under the principal control (see Appendix 1).

- Include more case studies or round table dialogue which include guidance on handling controversial issues.

- Create more opportunities to collaborate with other administration teams to brainstorm, share ideas, problem-solve, etc.

We need to realize more assistant principals becoming principals. Attrition rates alone tell us this—full stop! At the outset of this book, we spoke of how the research on the role and importance of assistant principals, over the course of the past 50 years, has called for more to be done to provide better, more practical development and leadership formation. Often left to the luck of the draw for mentorship and guidance, we stressed the idea that to attract more aspiring leaders to the mantle of principalship, more focused and intentional learning experiences are needed. In this book, we have provided a rooted approach which we firmly believe to be impactful on getting more assistant principals on the pathway to principalship.

It is our sincerest hope that this book has provided you with an array of ideas, strategies, and tools to better understand where your aspiring leaders are on their journey, how to encourage them to take next steps, and provide them with meaningful guided and mastery learning experiences. We know full well that the pathway is not without its challenges. Nonetheless, we need to help our principals and system leaders become stronger guides (mentors and coaches) to help shine light on the way ahead. We hold firmly to the impact that our four roots can have in better preparing our assistant principals to walk that tree-lined pathway. We conclude with these insightful and powerful words which for us, frame the true task at hand in attracting more aspiring leaders to the pathway to principalship: "People with high assurance in their capabilities approach difficult tasks as challenges to be mastered rather than as threats to be avoided" (Bandura, 1977, p. 11).

Hopefully, the end of this book won't mean the end of your learning. Some aspiring leaders may end up taking a longer pathway to principalship (more experiential learning, more vicarious learning experiences, more practical development to yield capacity realization), and that is ok! If you are a systems leader, you may want to consider how you can go further up the pathway to seek out potential aspiring leaders. If you are a building leader, you may want to continue to create leadership experiences for all aspiring leaders in your school. If you are reading this and you are an aspiring leader, it is our hope that you gleaned information that will guide you along the pathway to principalship and become Leader Ready!

AFTERWORD

Post-COVID, there have been numerous claims about school leaders burning out, feeling stressed, and burdened by an excessive workload. In the 2018 TALIS results for my country, Australia, 89% of leaders report administrative work as a major source of stress in government schools (Thomson & Hillman, 2020). Contrast this with these same principals (89%) reporting high levels of innovation and friendliness in their schools, 74% reporting they are satisfied with their salary, 84% are satisfied with other terms of their employment, 89% reporting higher rates of autonomy than the OECD average, and over 90% claiming job satisfaction. Specifically, "I enjoy working at this school" (96%), "All in all, I am satisfied with my job" (98%), "I would recommend this school as a good place to work" (98%), and "I am satisfied with my performance in this school" (93%). Furthermore, nearly all Australian principals would choose the role if starting anew (94%) and have no regrets about deciding to become a principal (97%).

How to resolve this seeming contradiction: high stress and workload and love of the job. Since the 1970s, psychological research has changed the focus on stress to coping strategies (Frydenberg, 2022). There are stressors, but our coping strategies (cognitive or emotional) allow us to deal with them. Moreover, the same stressors can invoke differential coping strategies. Indeed, this shows that principals must have remarkably high levels of coping strategies. Yes, it would be great to reduce the stressors, but the more critical claim is to point to remarkably high levels of resilience, coping, and skills to deal with them.

This book provides a clear focus on developing these coping strategies. It does not ignore the stressors, such as the ever-pressing compliance forms, the calls from parents, the HR issues and performance of staff, the seeking someone (anyone) to cover every class, and the responsibility for the learning, climate, culture, and achievement of students in the school. And that is but a start. The massive increase of middle leaders is aimed to ameliorate some of the pressures from leaders, but often this leads to more experiencing stressors—and more opportunity to venting and other not so effective emotional coping strategies (Productivity Commission, 2022).

The teaching supply problem in many countries post-COVID is tomorrow's leadership supply crisis. There does seem to be a trend to create even more middle leadership roles as systems try to find ways to remunerate teachers more while adding more roles and responsibilities (which does not help keep excellent teachers in the classroom). Further, the average age of first registering as a teacher in Australia is approaching 30. These new teachers are in their second or third career change and teaching may not be their last, they want to join a collaborative profession that values expertise, they look aghast at the declining increase in salary beyond 7–10 years as a teacher, and they see leaders dealing with difficult other teachers and students and wonder if that is the role for them.

The request in this book is for a "firm, clear vision," more attention to teaching implementation science, and developing confidence to take on the challenges and stressors of the role. They call their model "the Roots of School Leader Preparation," with four roots: higher leadership standards, creating a culture for implementation, planning guided leadership experiences, and attaining mastery experiences. It does surprise me when I ask leaders about their model of implementation. In other disciplines (e.g., medicine, engineering, policy, computing), there are many evidence-based implementation models (we identified over 50 with evidence of impact, Hamilton, Reeves, Clinton, & Hattie, 2022), and developing, adopting, and evaluating these models into education should be welcomed. So many great policies and ideas fail in the implementation phase. To then be resurrected (because they are good ideas) and tried again and again.

There is also the plea to raise the bar of leadership standards. First, they identify many standards, and six major components seem to dominate: Leading Mission, Vision, Culture, Equity, and Ethics; Leading teaching and learning; Leading collective efficacy for all in the school (including developing relations and high expectations); Leading the development of self and others (all adults and students in the school); Leading the management of the school; and Leading engagement with the community.

Unlike teaching in a class, many of these involve responsibility for other teachers' practice and performance, ensuring compliance with the system and society's rules, greater engagement with parents, and the skills of building high trust and collective expectations and impacts of all adults in the school. In a profession that values collaboration while at the same time privileging independent contractors (i.e., I have the autonomy to teach as I believe, I do not welcome other adults in my class to watch me, I respect you, so leave me alone), this can be difficult. Throughout this book, the contribution highlights the addition of the leader to engender collective efficacy across the school, particularly around ensuring high expectations.

It is also notable that in most lists of Standards, there is less attention to the standard within the Standard. There is also often no gradation with the implication that you are a great leader from Day one, that you do not grow as a leader, there is little developing expertise from becoming a leader, and there is a jump from being a teacher to being a leader. Recently there has been emerging debates about standards for Middle leaders (see NSW Department of Education, 2022; The Teacher Leaders Model Standards, 2020), but like many teacher standards where there are gradations (e.g., Australia has Graduate, Proficient, Highly Accomplished, and Lead), there also needs to be gradations in leader standards.

What is missing from most standards is the responsibility for building the system across many schools and at the system level. During COVID, for example, I know not one system in the world that created policies to help leaders or teachers teach online and hybrid. It was the collective impact of leaders talking to each other, teachers talking to each other, and the evidence of the average effect was quite minor compared to the workload, the pains, equity, death, unemployment etc. ($d = -0.15$; see König & Frey, 2022; Zierer, 2021). There could be powerful innovations in our education system if we could harness the power of educators to inform the system, rather than so often the top-down edict of policy. The OECD "new democracies" movement could be adapted to the development of education policy. The best school then should be the school next door, as school leaders work across schools stop claiming that their school is unique, but that there are many shared issues that the schools collective could resolve—and work upwards to inform the system.

In NSW, the politicians asked for a reconsideration of the career structure for teachers. Now, teachers hit a pay ceiling after seven years (after that, there is only cost of living increases), and many students do not consider teaching knowing this ceiling and that they will go backwards relative to other professions. The only major way to increase salary is to pluck the most successful teachers into leadership roles. Changing remuneration and career trajectories walks over a thousand past failures, so one of the strategies was to engage in the "new democracies" movement and build the policy from the schools up. A case for change paper was released and views of schools sought to lead into an Options paper (NSW Department, 2022). Over 100 Roundtables in every school network in the state is being held. From this the Options paper will morph into recommendations (and one option is Do not Do it), but if there is momentum, then a 2–4-year "test and learn" will be conducted in schools with an evaluation plan to inform the policy further before it is scaled up. Maybe a further standard should relate to developing leaders into systems leaders.

The book identifies various skills and dispositions to achieve the Standards. These include: discover the feel of the environment; engage in active listening; determine the skill, will, and thrill of your people; discern affective state; leverage social persuasion; and tailor feedback. I add one more: the leader's skill to stop doing things that are not working or adding little value. The first four actions relate to diagnosing the current situation and establishing the climate across the school. Sometimes leaders rush to action, pulling something out of their toolkit that worked for them (or someone else) in another context. My continual claim is that the greatest power of a leader is deciding and determining the narrative for the school. This leads to developing what

O'Leary calls the vibe of the school (O'Leary, 2022). Creating the culture and climate is the bedrock of leadership.

The skills are not collecting data, listening to others' views, and being open to the voices of the students and community—they are all important precursors *to making interpretations then deciding actions.* We underestimate the interpreting, the thinking, and the evaluative mindset that are crucial. Great leaders know when to listen and when to talk, when to wait and when to act, when to delegate when to do it themselves, when to report and when to stay silent. This Kenny Rogers leadership model (Know when to play 'em, Know when to hold 'em) is often overlooked in the skills of leaders. We so often emphasize the language, the talk, and the direction from leaders and ignore the listening skills. As noted in Chapter 3, the skill is better considered as "active listening." Demonstrating you not only heard but understood—but this does not mean you agree. This section of the book is worth the purchase price in itself. What greater mark of respect to other teachers (and students) than demonstrating active listening.

So many leadership books ignore or gloss over the management role—the management of compliance, budgets, and especially people (the hardest of all roles). Such SKILLS sit along the more exciting attributes of leadership, but these skills are the basics—if not done well, disaster is imminent. The highest WILL attribute is confidence to take on challenges, and I recite the last line in the book: "People with high assurance in their capabilities approach difficult tasks as challenges to be mastered rather than as threats to be avoided" (Bandura, 1977, p. 11). The highest THRILL is knowing, enabling, and convincing all that every student—no matter their prior achievement or background—can make at least a year's growth for a year's input. This expectation of at least a year's growth needs transparent articulation, evidence of the growth, expectations that it can be done in this school by all, and needs esteem and joy when it is accomplished. "Growth" can include achievement, development of learning strategies, respect for self and others, turning on and engaging in learning, physical and artistic progress, and feeling invited and wanting to come to school to learn what we teach our students. These all beg the question of the major focus for leaders. I would argue that this vision of at least a year's growth is a primary mission, but the leader's major influence is then the culture and climate of the staff room and classroom to make this happen—what Tim and Vince call the "culture for implementation."

Becoming a principal requires confidence, skills, motivation, and a passion for spreading your sphere of influence beyond the classroom. As noted above, it is a position that commands respect, is rewarding, and demands high levels of coping strategies.

—**Professor John Hattie**

APPENDICES

Appendix 1: Research on the Self-Efficacy of Assistant Principals

Appendix 2: Comparing Leadership Standards

Appendix 3: Universal Leadership Standard (ULS) Inventory

Appendix 4: Levels of Experience Template

Appendix 5: Feedback Template for Skill, Will, and Thrill

Appendix 6: Culminating Activity: Leadership Growth Plan Template

APPENDIX 1

Research on the Self-Efficacy of Assistant Principals

For further information on the research regarding the efficacy of assistant principals, please consider looking through Dr. Tim Cusack's doctoral dissertation. Inspiration for this book stems from research conducted over the span of 2017–2020. Below you will find a link to Cusack's (2020) dissertation

that expands on aspects of self-efficacy, leadership standard, social cognitive learning theory, and the detailed perspectives of assistant principals and their desire to move into principalship. We have provided the abstract of the study for more information: https://www.proquest.com/openview/dc77341ed00c63058bef862075e26981/1?pq-origsite=gscholar&cbl=18750&diss=y.

Abstract

This study sought to understand the perceived levels of managerial, instructional, and moral self-efficacy of assistant principals ($N = 101$) serving in an urban Albertan school jurisdiction. Levels of self-efficacy (Bandura, 1986) were measured using the Principal Sense of Efficacy Scale (PSES) (Tschannen-Moran & Gareis, 2004). Additionally, the instructional leadership indicators of the Alberta Leader Quality Standard (LQS) (Alberta Education, 2019) were measured for levels of importance and perceived level of proficiency by participants. Finally, assistant principals were asked to indicate if they held aspirations for principalship, provide rationale for their response, and express what professional learning experiences might be necessary to become a principal.

This study contributed to the extant literature pertaining to building and realizing greater levels of self-efficacy in assistant principals, a population which has been chronically underserved and underrepresented in the literature. Existing research has suggested that more time and attention is needed in the domain of instructional leadership which is often overlooked due to the managerial demands of an administrative role that has not been fully defined appreciated, or supported.

The first phase of this study analyzed the PSES scores across three subscales and found that participants scored highest in efficacy for moral leadership second highest in instructional, and lowest in managerial. These results were disaggregated by various demographic factors and suggested that females ($n = 70$) had the highest scores in all subscales compared to males ($n = 31$). The second phase of the research design asked participants to rate levels of importance and proficiency on the nine indicators inherent to the LQS instructional leadership domain. In both importance and proficiency, it was males who scored higher than females. A very strong correlation of $r = .93$ was found between the level of importance and level of proficiency across all participants. Relationships between the PSES instructional subscale and the LQS indicators revealed a stronger relationship for females $r = .48$ than males ($r = .40$).

Finally, 33% of participants indicated aspirations to pursue principalship whereas 21% did not and the remainder were undecided. Ongoing long-term mentorship, more mastery learning experiences in instructional leadership, and leading the operations of a learning community were among the top responses from the participants as to what is needed to further their professional development.

This descriptive study sought to understand the landscape of assistant principals in an urban setting and how their self-efficacy scores and interaction with leadership standards (instructional leadership) might provide the school jurisdiction with insights on how to enhance existing assistant principal leadership programming.

APPENDIX 2

Comparing Leadership Standards

What are your local standards? We have left some space below for you to jot down your local standards and have included our Universal Leadership Standards (ULS) in a column for you to compare. Where might each of your standards align with the ULS?

YOUR LOCAL STANDARDS	UNIVERSAL LEADERSHIP STANDARDS
	• Learning and Engagement
	• Resources and Operations
	• Community and Culture
	• Growth and Innovation

APPENDIX 3

Universal Leadership Standard (ULS) Inventory

Universal Leadership Standard (ULS) Inventory of Assistant Principal Self-Efficacy

Read the following prompts and rate "to what extent in your role as assistant principal" you agree with each statement below. Note that a score of 1 means "not at all"/3 means "a little bit"/5 means "somewhat"/7 means "a good amount"/and 9 means "a great amount."

Note: We recommend using the full 24 question version with your cadre of assistant principals to get a sense of overall capacity. Ideally you would collect these data in Spring for purposes of Fall planning. The next four pages provide the Inventory of Assistant Principal Capacity separated into each of the four ULS categories. This will allow you to examine the six corresponding questions for each category.

1. I can lead meaningful professional learning activities with staff.

1	2	3	4	5	6	7	8	9

2. I have opportunity to engage in school finances (budgeting) and resource management.

1	2	3	4	5	6	7	8	9

3. I can engage students, parents, guardians, and stakeholders in celebrating aspects of school culture and success.

1	2	3	4	5	6	7	8	9

4. I have opportunity to propose new initiatives and processes in support of enhancing student and staff learning.

1	2	3	4	5	6	7	8	9

5. I model high-impact assessment practices for teachers.

1	2	3	4	5	6	7	8	9

6. I participate in staffing and hiring processes at my school.

1	2	3	4	5	6	7	8	9

7. I can promote respectful relationships among students, staff, and stakeholders.

1	2	3	4	5	6	7	8	9

8. I can create an environment open to inquiry, experiment, original thinking, and risk-taking.

1	2	3	4	5	6	7	8	9

9. I can interpret and leverage an array of divisional data sources.

1	2	3	4	5	6	7	8	9

10. I can interpret and ethically apply policy and procedural frameworks pertaining to teaching and learning.

1	2	3	4	5	6	7	8	9

11. I have opportunities to promote the values and vision of the school and jurisdiction to the local and wider community.

1	2	3	4	5	6	7	8	9

12. I have opportunities to access ongoing job-embedded professional development in leadership or areas of academic interest.

1	2	3	4	5	6	7	8	9

13. I can provide high quality supervision of teachers and staff.

1	2	3	4	5	6	7	8	9

14. I have opportunity to provide quality input into physical infrastructure needs.

1	2	3	4	5	6	7	8	9

15. I am able to respond to community needs in a proactive and timely fashion.

1	2	3	4	5	6	7	8	9

16. I encourage cross-curricular collaboration and teacher creativity in deepening academic press.

1	2	3	4	5	6	7	8	9

17. I promote a culture that is caring, welcoming, and inclusive.

| 1 | 2 | 3 | 4 | 5 | 6 | 7 | 8 | 9 |

18. I can identify and address operational needs and challenges.

| 1 | 2 | 3 | 4 | 5 | 6 | 7 | 8 | 9 |

19. I have opportunities to facilitate community engagement activities.

| 1 | 2 | 3 | 4 | 5 | 6 | 7 | 8 | 9 |

20. I have opportunities to contribute to the creation of school plans for continuous growth.

| 1 | 2 | 3 | 4 | 5 | 6 | 7 | 8 | 9 |

21. I am well versed in the curricular resources available to support student learning.

| 1 | 2 | 3 | 4 | 5 | 6 | 7 | 8 | 9 |

22. I am able to promote occupational health, wellness, and safety in the workplace.

| 1 | 2 | 3 | 4 | 5 | 6 | 7 | 8 | 9 |

23. I have training in equity, diversity, inclusion, and cultural sensitivity.

1	2	3	4	5	6	7	8	9

24. I can facilitate meaningful dialogue and processes to promote teacher professional growth.

1	2	3	4	5	6	7	8	9

Scoring:

To determine sense of self-efficacy for each area of the 4 ULS, do the following:

Learning and Engagement: Get the sum of items: 1, 5, 9, 13, 17, and 21. Divide by 6.

Resources and Operations: Get the sum of items: 2, 6, 10, 14, 18, and 22. Divide by 6.

Community and Culture: Get the sum of items: 3, 7, 11, 15, 19, and 23. Divide by 6.

Growth and Innovation: Get the sum of items: 4, 8, 12, 16, 20, and 24. Divide by 6.

For a full-scale score: Get the sum of all 24 items and divide by 24.

Inventory of Assistant Principal Capacity (Learning and Engagement)

Read the following prompts and rate "to what extent" your jurisdiction (or school) leadership training programming places emphasis, focus, or priority on the topic at hand. Note that a score of 1 means "not at all"/3 means "a little bit"/5 means "somewhat"/7 means "a good amount"/and 9 means "a great amount."

1. I can lead meaningful professional learning activities with staff.

1	2	3	4	5	6	7	8	9

2. I model high-impact assessment practices for teachers.

1	2	3	4	5	6	7	8	9

3. I can interpret and leverage an array of divisional data sources.

1	2	3	4	5	6	7	8	9

4. I can provide high-quality supervision of teachers and staff.

1	2	3	4	5	6	7	8	9

5. I promote a culture that is caring, welcoming, and inclusive.

1	2	3	4	5	6	7	8	9

6. I am well versed in the curricular resources available to support student learning.

1	2	3	4	5	6	7	8	9

Scoring: Find the sum of the six questions and divide by 6.

Inventory of Assistant Principal Capacity (Resources and Operations)

Read the following prompts and rate "to what extent" your jurisdiction (or school) leadership training programming places emphasis, focus, or priority on the topic at hand. Note that a score of 1 means "not at all"/3 means "a little bit"/ 5 means "somewhat"/7 means "a good amount"/and 9 means "a great amount."

1. I have opportunity to engage in school finances (budgeting) and resource management.

1	2	3	4	5	6	7	8	9

2. I participate in staffing and hiring processes at my school.

1	2	3	4	5	6	7	8	9

3. I can interpret and ethically apply policy and procedural frameworks pertaining to teaching and learning.

1	2	3	4	5	6	7	8	9

4. I have opportunity to provide quality input into physical infrastructure needs.

1	2	3	4	5	6	7	8	9

5. I can identify and address operational needs and challenges.

1	2	3	4	5	6	7	8	9

6. I am able to promote occupational health, wellness, and safety in the workplace.

1	2	3	4	5	6	7	8	9

Scoring: Find the sum of the six questions and divide by 6.

Read the following prompts and rate "to what extent" your jurisdiction (or school) leadership training programming places emphasis, focus, or priority on the topic at hand. Note that a score of 1 means "not at all"/3 means "a little bit"/ 5 means "somewhat"/7 means "a good amount"/and 9 means "a great amount."

1. I have the opportunity to engage students, parents, guardians, and stakeholders in celebrating aspects of school culture and success.

1	2	3	4	5	6	7	8	9

2. I am able to promote respectful relationships among students, staff, and stakeholders.

1	2	3	4	5	6	7	8	9

3. I have opportunities to promote the values and vision of the school and jurisdiction to the local and wider community.

1	2	3	4	5	6	7	8	9

4. I am able to respond to community needs in a proactive and timely fashion.

1	2	3	4	5	6	7	8	9

5. I have opportunities to facilitate community engagement activities.

1	2	3	4	5	6	7	8	9

6. I have training in equity, diversity, inclusion, and cultural sensitivity.

1	2	3	4	5	6	7	8	9

Scoring: Find the sum of the six questions and divide by 6.

Inventory of Assistant Principal Capacity (Growth and Innovation)

Read the following prompts and rate "to what extent" your jurisdiction (or school) leadership training programming places emphasis, focus, or priority on the topic at hand. Note that a score of 1 means "not at all"/3 means "a little bit"/ 5 means "somewhat"/7 means "a good amount"/and 9 means "a great amount."

1. I have opportunity to propose new initiatives and processes in support of enhancing student and staff learning.

1	2	3	4	5	6	7	8	9

2. I can create an environment open to inquiry, experiment, original thinking, and risk-taking.

1	2	3	4	5	6	7	8	9

3. I have opportunities to access ongoing job-embedded professional development in leadership or areas of academic interest.

1	2	3	4	5	6	7	8	9

4. I encourage cross-curricular collaboration and teacher creativity in deepening academic press.

1	2	3	4	5	6	7	8	9

5. I have opportunities to contribute to the creation of school plans for continuous growth.

1	2	3	4	5	6	7	8	9

6. I can facilitate meaningful dialogue and processes to promote teacher professional growth.

1	2	3	4	5	6	7	8	9

Scoring: Find the sum of the six questions and divide by 6.

APPENDIX 4

Levels of Experience Template

Use this blank Levels of Experience template to create leveled experiences in an area of need that you've identified for your assistant principals. Fill in a new template for each area of need you have identified. You can access a printable PDF of this template on this book's resource page at https://us.corwin.com/books/leader-ready-281684.

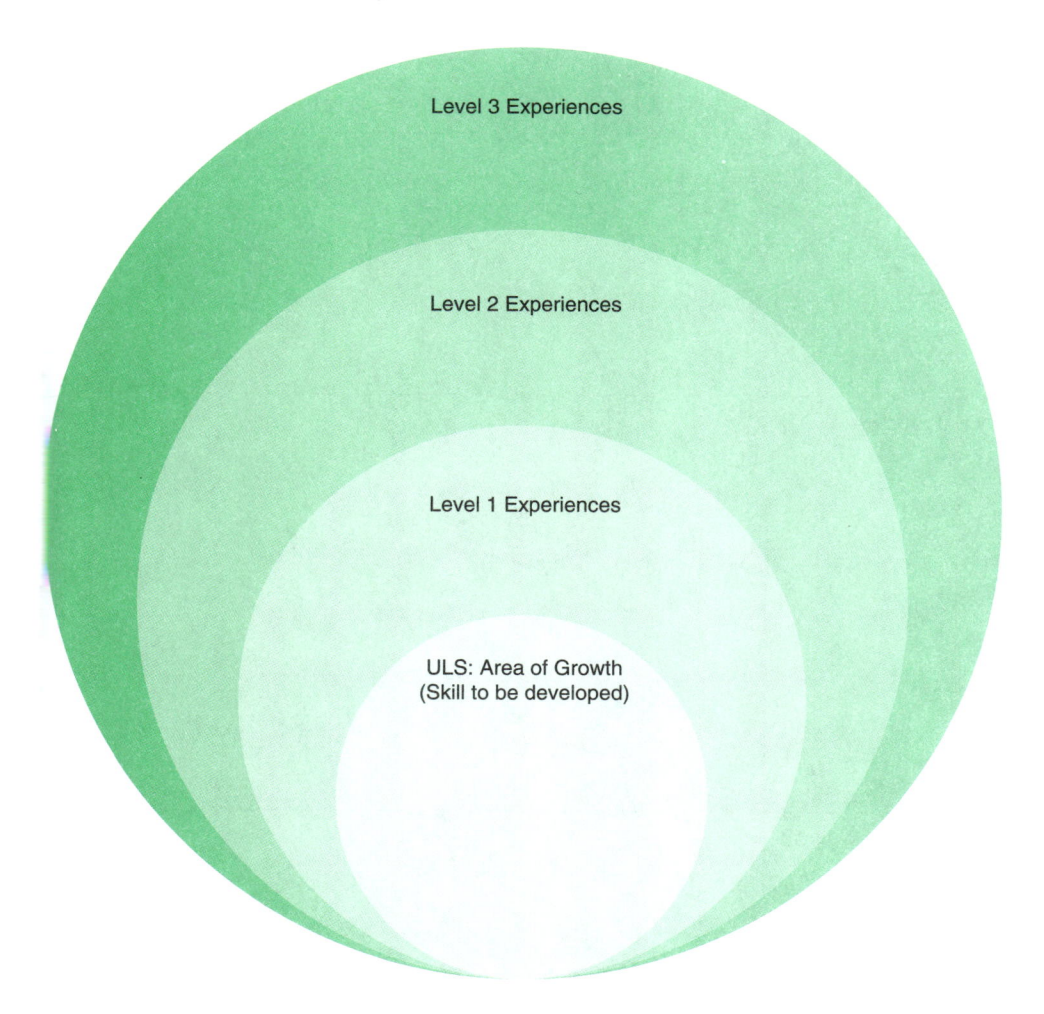

Level 3 Experiences

Level 2 Experiences

Level 1 Experiences

ULS: Area of Growth
(Skill to be developed)

Feedback Template for Skill, Will, and Thrill

In Chapter 5, we discussed the importance of feedback in generating mastery experiences. Use the template below to craft specific feedback stems for coaching aspiring leaders through the development of their skill, will, and thrill.

Feedback for Skill	
Feedback for Will	
Feedback for Thrill	

APPENDIX 6

Culminating Activity: Leadership Growth Plan Template

As a culmination of the information presented in our book, we wanted to provide you with a practical model that you can use as a leadership template. This template can be used by aspiring school leaders, assistant principals, and principals alike. The purpose of the template is to use our ULS as goals in which we can design leadership learning experiences to track our growth. We left space for multiple ULS to be addressed and this template will also be available in a PDF document for you to use. As a guide, we have also included two examples (one from an assistant principal and one from a principal) to help guide your process.

Leadership Growth Plan

Name:

School:

Date:

Leadership Context: Describe your current reality. What is your portfolio? What professional learning experiences do you think are needed or would be value-added this year? Aim to write one or two paragraphs.

Self-Reflection: Provide context on your leadership journey thus far. What is important to you? What are some key aspects or beliefs about leadership you want to affirm or challenge? Based on leadership standards, what are your areas identified for growth for the upcoming year? Aim to write one or two paragraphs.

ULS #1 Goal:				
Skill, Will, and Thrill Development:	Specific Experiences for Focus (e.g., Skills to Build)	Resources That Will Help	Timeline for Completion (Include Key Dates/ Timings)	Measures or Indicators of Success
Level 1 Experiences				
Level 2 Experiences				
Level 3 Experiences				
Why is this goal significant to you?				

ULS #2

Goal:

Skill, Will, and Thrill Development:	Specific Experiences for Focus (e.g., Skills to Build)	Resources That Will Help	Timeline for Completion (Include Key Dates/ Timings)	Measures or Indicators of Success
Level 1 Experiences				
Level 2 Experiences				
Level 3 Experiences				

Why is this goal significant to you?

ULS #3

Goal:

Skill, Will, and Thrill Development:	Specific Experiences for Focus (e.g., Skills to Build)	Resources That Will Help	Timeline for Completion (Include Key Dates/ Timings)	Measures or Indicators of Success
Level 1 Experiences				
Level 2 Experiences				
Level 3 Experiences				

Why is this goal significant to you?

ULS #4

Goal:

Skill, Will, and Thrill Development:	Specific Experiences for Focus (e.g., Skills to Build)	Resources That Will Help	Timeline for Completion (Include Key Dates/ Timings)	Measures or Indicators of Success
Level 1 Experiences				
Level 2 Experiences				
Level 3 Experiences				

Why is this goal significant to you?

ULS:

Learning and Engagement: This leadership standard reflects all capacities of instructional leadership. This may include decisions that directly impact the students, staff, and community stakeholders. Leaders who implement this standard acknowledge the impact of high-quality instruction on student learning and achievement.

GOAL:

During the school year, I will lead staff through instructional/pedagogical professional learning to build my capacity as an instructional leader.

Skill, Will, and Thrill Development:	Specific Experiences for Focus (e.g., Skills to Build)	Resources That Will Help	Timeline for Completion (Include Key Dates/Timings)	Measures or Indicators of Success
Level 1 Experiences	Attend professional learning conferences or workshops	– Professional learning conferences that link to school growth plans – Books, webinars, colleagues to reflect on the impact of professional learning	– Yearlong with expectation to attend professional learning experiences continually throughout the year	– I will be able to report back to my principal the main focus of the professional learning sessions as they relate to our school goals
Level 2 Experiences	Facilitate professional learning experiences with staff	– District support team (to assist with facilitation) – Principal/mentor to provide support and feedback – Books, professional learning materials to support facilitation	– Midyear: November–December (to have an opportunity to get feedback and repeat the facilitation process)	– Staff is receptive to the professional learning I have selected and facilitated – Feedback and conversations with the principal are positive – School staff are receptive to professional learning and begin implementation
Level 3 Experiences	Lead school through a professional learning workshop	– District support team (for professional learning support) – Principal/mentor to provide support and feedback – Books, professional learning materials to support facilitation	– Late school year or when the principal determines competency to move to this step	– Professional learning workshops are created and facilitated independently – School staff are receptive to professional learning and implementation is ongoing – Feedback from school staff and principal is positive

Sample Goal Setting Plan From a Principal Mentoring New Assistant Principals

ULS: Operations and Resources

GOAL: During this school year, I will work with my assistant principal to increase their self-efficacy in the management and facilitation of the school emergency response portfolio.

Skill, Will, and Thrill Development:	Specific Experiences for Focus (e.g., Skills to Build)	Resources That Will Help	Timeline for Completion (Include Key Dates/Timings)	Measures or Indicators of Success
Level 1 Experiences	– Read district policy/procedures on Fire drill, Lockdown, First aid, severe weather, and other emergency scenarios – Observe current practices for all required drills/practices	– Corresponding policy/procedure documents/State protocols – Local resource supports, e.g., police, fire, medical, other government agencies, etc. Connect with division safety officer to discuss current practices and standards	August–September (review at weekly team meetings) Monthly or as required connections with safety officer or other relevant stakeholders, e.g., local police resource officer	– AP knows where to find all pertinent documents and information regarding school-based emergency response – AP can articulate who local resource support personnel are and knows how to contact/access supports when needed
Level 2 Experiences	Participate in a series of planned static emergency drills under principal supervision/guidance. This will see an increase in the level of responsibility to take on more lead role in the conducting of dynamic drills	Ongoing discussions of various scenarios, e.g., a simultaneous fire/Lockdown External stakeholder feedback, e.g., police/fire chief Discussion with other AP colleagues at PD (Professional Development) sessions	* September—Shadow principal in initial fire drill and lock down practices * October–November—Assign AP specific role in executing the various drills (debrief accordingly) * December–January—Initiate drills with principal shadowing/coaching	– AP can discuss all salient components of various emergency procedures – AP can lead aspects of the drill, e.g., fire warden for a certain sector of school – AP can organize a practice drill and lead with principal support including required reporting and documentation
Level 3 Experiences	AP leads both static and dynamic drills (scheduled and unannounced) AP can assume emergency response as part of admin portfolio	Feedback as required from principal and other stakeholders Opportunity to communicate school-based operations to district	February–June	AP can organize, schedule, and execute all required drills. AP can draft and share salient reports to district leadership AP can lead learning in this area for onboarding new staff

REFERENCES

Abu Dhabi Education Council. (2018). *Professional standards for principals.*

Alberta Education. (2009). *Principal quality practice guideline: Promoting successful school leadership in Alberta.* Edmonton, AB: Author.

Alberta Education. (2013). *Teaching and Learning International Survey (TALIS) 2013.* Edmonton, AB: Author.

Alberta Education. (2018). *Leadership quality standard.* Edmonton, AB: Alberta Government. Retrieved from https://education.alberta.ca/media/3739621/standardsdoc-lqs-_fa-web-2018-01-17.pdf

Alberta Education. (2019). *Leadership quality standard.* Edmonton, AB: Alberta Government.

Alberta Teachers' Association. (2019). *Authority and role of administrators.* Retrieved from https://www.teachers.ab.ca/News%20Room/Publications/Teachers%20%20Rights%20Responsibilities%20and%20Legal%20Liabilities/Pages/Chapter%207.aspx

Alberta Teachers' Retirement Fund. (2017). *Looking forward to your future: 2017 annual report.* Retrieved from https://atrf.com/Publications/2017AnnualReport_FinancialStatements.pdf

Armstrong, D. (2009). *Administrative passages: Navigating the transition from teaching to administration.* Dordrecht: Springer-Verlag.

Armstrong, D. (2010). Rites of passage: Coercion, compliance, and complicity in the socialization of new vice-principals. *Teachers College Record, 112*(3), 685–722.

Armstrong, D. (2012). Connecting personal change and organizational passage in the transition from teacher to vice principal. *Journal of School Leadership, 22,* 398–425.

Armstrong, D. (2014, April). *Transition to the role of principal and vice principal study.* Retrieved from https://education leadership-ontario.ca

Armstrong, D. (2015). Listening to voices at the educational frontline: New administrators' experiences of the transition from teacher to vice-principal. *Brock Education Journal, 24*(2), 109–122.

Armstrong, D. E. (2005). Leadership at the crossroads: Negotiating challenges, tensions, and ambiguities in the transition from teaching to administration. In H. D. Armstrong (Ed.), *Examining the practice of school administration in Canada* (pp. 113–128). Calgary, AB: Detselig Enterprises.

Augustine-Shaw, D., & Liang, J. (2016). Embracing new realities: Professional growth for new principals and mentors. *Educational Considerations, 43*(3), 10–17. doi:10.4148/0146-9282.1016

Austin, D., & Brown, H. (1970). Report on the assistant principalship. In *The study of the secondary principalship* (*Vol. 3*). Washington, DC: National Association of Secondary School Principals.

Australian Institute for Teaching and School Leadership. (2014). *Australian professional standard for principals and the leadership profiles.* Melbourne, VIC: Australian Institute for Teaching and School Leadership.

Australian Institute for Teaching and School Leadership. (2015). *Preparing future leaders: Effective preparation for aspiring school principals.* Melbourne, VIC: Australian Institute for Teaching and School Leadership.

Australian Institute for Teaching and School Leadership. (2016). *Evaluating your principal preparation programs: A practical guide*. Melbourne, VIC: Australian Institute for Teaching and School Leadership.

Babo, G., & Ramaswami, S. (2016, Spring). New Jersey principals' perceptions on the application and importance of the ISLLC 2008 standards' "functions:" A preferred hierarchy. *Journal for Leadership and Instruction, Spring*, 12–16.

Bandura, A. (1977). *Social learning theory*. Englewood Cliffs, NJ: Prentice Hall.

Bandura, A. (1986). *Social foundations of thought and action: A social cognitive theory*. Englewood Cliffs, NJ: Prentice-Hall.

Bandura, A. (1994). Self-efficacy. In V. S. Ramachaudran (Ed.), *Encyclopedia of human behavior* (*Vol. 4*, pp. 71–81). New York, NY: Academic Press. Reprinted in H. Friedman (Ed.), *Encyclopedia of mental health*. San Diego: Academic Press, 1998.

Bandura, A. (1997). *Self-efficacy: The exercise of control*. New York, NY: Freeman.

Bandura, A. (2001). Guide for constructing self-efficacy scales. In G. V. Caprara (Ed.), *La valutazione dell 'autoeffcacia [The assessment of self-efficacy]* (pp. 15–37). Trento: Erickson.

Bandura, A. (2009). Cultivate self-efficacy for personal and organizational effectiveness. In E. A. Locke (Ed.), *Handbook of principles of organization behavior* (2nd ed., pp. 179–200). New York, NY: Wiley.

Bandura, A. (2012). On the functional properties of perceived self-efficacy revisited. *Journal of Management, 38*, 9–44.

Barnett, B. G., Shoho, A. R., & Oleszewski, A. (2012). The job realities of beginning and experienced assistant principals. *Leadership and Policy in Schools, 11*(1), 92–128.

California County Superintendents Educational Services Association. (2016). *Best practices in teacher and administrator induction programs*. Arlington, VA: Hanover Research. Retrieved from http://ccsesa.org/wp-content/uploads/2016/06/Best-Practices-in-Teacher-and-Administrator-Induction-Programs.pdf

Center for Creative Leadership. (2020). *How to give the most effective feedback*. https://www.ccl.org/articles/leading-effe-ctively-articles/review-time-how-to-give-different-types-of-feedback/

Coates, S. M. (2020). *Pathways to the superintendency: The experiences of Albertan female superintendents* (p. 77). Graduate Theses and Dissertations. Retrieved from https://pilotscholars.up.edu/etd/77

Council of Chief State School Officers (CCSSO). (2015). *Model principal supervisor professional standards 2015*. Washington, DC: CCSSO.

Craft, H., Malveaux, R., Lopez, S., & Combs, J. (2016). The acclimation of new assistant principals. *Journal of School Administration Research and Development, 1*(2), 9–18.

Crown. (2020). Department for education. *Headteachers' Standards*. Retrieved from https://www.gov.uk/government/publications/national-standards-of-excellence-for-headteachers/headteachers-standards-2020. Accessed on 2 March 2022.

Cusack, T. P. (2020). *Understanding the self-efficacy of assistant principals in an urban school division: Patterns, trends, and challenges to be mastered* (p. 72). Graduate Theses and Dissertations. Retrieved from https://pilotscholars.up.edu/etd/72

Dahlkamp, S., Peters, M., & Schumacher, G. (2017). Principal self-efficacy, school climate, and teacher retention: A multi-level analysis. *Alberta Journal of Educational Research, 63*(4), 357–376.

Darling-Hammond, L. (2007). Excellent teachers deserve excellent leaders. In *Education leadership: A bridge to school reform* (p. 17). New York, NY: The Wallace Foundation.

Darling-Hammond, L., Meyerson, D., LaPointe, M. T., & Orr, M. (2010). *Preparing principals for a changing world: Lessons from effective school leadership programs*. San Francisco, CA: Jossey-Bass.

Davis, S., Darling-Hammond, L., LaPointe, M., & Meyerson, D. (2005). *School leadership study: Developing successful principals*. Stanford, CA: Stanford Educational Leadership Institute.

DeWitt, P. (2016). *Collaborative leadership: The six influences that matter most*. Thousand Oaks, CA: Corwin.

DeWitt, P. (2021). *Collective leader efficacy: Strengthening instructional leadership teams*. Thousand Oaks, CA: Corwin.

DeWitt, P. (2022). *De-implementation: Creating space to focus on what works.* Thousand Oaks, CA: Corwin.

Dhliwayo, M. (n.d.). *goodreads.com.* Retrieved from https://www.goodreads.com/quotes/8920706-if-a-tree-has-strong-roots-not-even-the-strongest. Accessed on 10 June 2022.

Dimmock, C., & Hattie, J. (1996). School principals' self-efficacy and its measurement in the context of restructuring. *School Effectiveness and School Improvement, 7*(1), 62–75.

Dinham, S., Collarbone, P., Evans, M., & Mackay, A. (2013). The development, endorsement and adoption of a national standard for principals in Australia. *Educational Management Administration & Leadership, 41*(4), 467–483.

Donohoo, J. (2017). *Collective efficacy: How educators' beliefs impact student learning.* Thousand Oaks, CA: Corwin.

Federici, R., & Skaalvik, E. (2011). Principal self-efficacy and work engagement: Assessing a Norwegian principal self-efficacy scale. *Social Psychology Education, 14,* 575–600.

Fink, D. (2011). Pipelines, pools and reservoirs: Building leadership capacity for sustained improvement. *Journal of Educational Administration, 49*(6), 670–684. doi: 10.1108/09578231111174811

Fisher, D., & Frey, N. (2014). *Better learning through structured teaching: A framework for the gradual release of responsibility.* Alexandria, VA: ASCD.

Frydenberg, E. (2022). *Coping in good times and bad.* Melbourne, VIC: Melbourne University Press.

Fullan, M. (2018). The principalship has changed: 2020 here we come! *Principal Connections, 22*(1), 18–19.

Fulton, O. K. (1987). Basic competencies of the assistant principal. *NASSP Bulletin, 71*(501), 52–54.

Gentilucci, J., Denti, L., & Guaglianone, C. (2013). New principals' perspectives of their multifaceted roles. *Educational Leadership and Administration: Teaching and Program Development, 24,* 75–85.

Glanz, J. (1994). Redefining the roles and responsibilities of assistant principals. *Clearing House, 7*(5), 283–287.

Goddard, R. D., Hoy, W. K., & Hoy, A. W. (2004). Collective efficacy beliefs: Theoretical developments, empirical evidence, and future directions. *Educational Researcher, 33*(3), 3–13.

Goddard, R. D., Hoy, W. K., & Woolfolk Hoy, A. (2000). Collective teacher efficacy: Its meaning, measure, and impact on student achievement. *American Educational Research Journal, 37,* 479–508.

Goldring, R., & Taie, S. (2018). *Principal attrition and mobility: Results from the 2016–17 principal followup survey first look (NCES 2018-066)* U.S. Department of Education. Washington, DC: National Center for Education Statistics. Retrieved from https://nces.ed.gov/pubsearch

Gonzalez, M. M. (2016). The coding manual for qualitative research: A review. *The Qualitative Report, 21*(8), 1546–1548. Retrieved from http://nsuworks.nova.edu/tqr/vol21/iss8/15

Grant, C., & Osanloo, A. (2014). Understanding, selecting, and integrating a theoretical framework in dissertation research: Creating the blueprint for your "house." *Admini-strative Issues Journal: Connecting Education, Practice, and Research, 4*(2), 12–16.

Grissom, J., & Loeb, S. (2009). *Triangulating principal effectiveness: How perspectives of parents, teachers, and assistant principals identify the central importance of managerial skills.* CALDER Working Paper 35. Washington, DC: The Urban Institute.

Grissom, J. A., & Loeb, S. (2011). Triangulating principal effectiveness: How perspectives of parents, teachers, and assistant principals identify the central importance of managerial skills. *American Educational Research Journal, 48*(5), 1091–1123.

Grodzki, J. (2011). Role identity: At the intersection of organizational socialization and individual sensemaking of new principals and vice-principals. *Canadian Journal of Educational Administration and Policy, 127,* 1–46.

Gurley, D., Anast-May, L., & Lee, T. (2015). Developing instructional leaders through assistant principals' academy: A partnership for success. *Education and Urban Society, 47*(2), 207–241.

Haller, A., Hunt, E., Pacha, J., & Fazekas, A. (2016). *Lessons for states: Every student succeeds act (ESSA) increases focus on and investment in supporting principal preparation and development.* Normal, IL: Illinois State University, Center for the Study of Education Policy.

Hamilton, A., Reeves, D. B., Clinton, J. M., & Hattie, J. (2022). *Building to impact: The 5D implementation playbook for educators.* Thousand Oaks, CA: Corwin.

Harris, S., & Lowery, S. (2003). *Standards-based leadership: A case study book for the principalship.* Lanham, MD: Scarecrow Education.

Hartzell, G. N. (1993). The assistant principal: Neglected actor in practitioner leadership literature. *Journal of School Leadership, 3*(6), 707–723.

Hattie, J. (2015). *What works best in education: The politics of collaborative expertise.* London: Pearson.

Hattie, J., Bustamante, V., Almarode, J., Fisher, D., & Frey, N. (2020). *Great teaching by design: From intention to implementation in the visible learning classroom.* Thousand Oaks, CA: Corwin.

Hattie, J., & Donoghue, G. (2016). Learning strategies: A synthesis and conceptual model. *Npj Science of Learning, 1,* 16013. doi:10.1038/npjscilearn.2016.13

Hoerr, T. (2005). *The art of school leadership.* Alexandria, VA: Association for Supervision and Curriculum Development.

Institute for Education Leadership. (2013). *The Ontario leadership framework: A school and system leader's guide to putting Ontario's leadership framework into practice.* Toronto, ON: Author.

Jalal ad-Din Muhammad Rumi (n.d.). *good reads.com.* Retrieved from https://www.goodreads.com/quotes/616306-maybe-you-are-searching-among-the-branches-for-what-only. Accessed on 10 June 2022.

Jensen, B., Hunter, A., Lambert, & Clark, A. (2015). *Aspiring principal preparation, prepared for the Australian Institute for Teaching and School Leadership.* Melbourne, VIC: AITSL.

König, C., & Frey, A. (2022). The impact of COVID-19-related school closures on student achievement—A meta-analysis. *Educational Measurement: Issues and Practice, 41*(1), 16–22.

Lehman, L., Boyland, L., & Sriver, S. (2014). Superintendents' perceptions of the effectiveness of newly hired principals. *International Journal of Educational Leadership Preparation, 9*(2), 91–110.

Leithwood, K. (2012). *The Ontario leadership framework, with a discussion of the research foundations.* Toronto, ON: Institute for Education Leadership.

Leithwood, K., & Mascall, B. (2003). Collective leadership effects on student achievement. *Educational Administration Quarterly, 44*(4), 529–561.

Levin, S., Scott, C., Yang, M., Leung, M., & Bradley, K. (2020). *Supporting a strong, stable principal workforce: What matters and what can be done.* Research report.

Levine, A. (2005). *Educating school leaders.* Retrieved from http://www.edschools.org/. Accessed on 16 June 2022.

Liu, S., Xu, X., Grant, L., Strong, J., & Fang, Z. (2015). Professional standards and performance evaluation for principals in China: A policy analysis of the development of principal standards. *Education Management Administration & Leadership, 45*(2), 238–259.

Marshall, C. (1992). Assistant principalship: An overview of the frustrations and rewards. *NASSP Bulletin, 76,* 88–94.

Marshall, C. (1993). *The unsung role of the career assistant principal.* Reston, VA: National Association of Secondary School Principals.

Marshall, C., & Greenfield, W. (1987). The dynamics in the enculturation and the work in assistant principalship. *Urban Education, 22,* 36–52.

Marzano, R. (2003). *What works in schools: Translating research into action.* Alexandria, VA: Association for Supervision and Curriculum Development.

McCormick, M. J. (2001). Self-efficacy and leadership effectiveness: Applying social cognitive theory to leadership. *Journal of Leadership Studies, 8*(1), 22–33.

Merler, M. (2010, January 22). Advocating for BCPVPA members. *British Columbia Principals' and Vice Principals' Association Newsletter,* pp. 1–3.

Morgan, T. (2018). Assistant principal's perceptions of the principalship. *International Journal of Education Policy & Leadership, 13*(10), 1–21.

Murphy, J. (2017). *Professional standards for educational leaders: The empirical, moral, and experiential foundations.* Thousand Oaks, CA: Corwin.

National Policy Board for Educational Administration. (2015). *Professional standards for educational leaders 2015.* Reston, VA. Retrieved from https://www.npbea.org/wp-content/uploads/2017/06/Professional-Standards-for-Educational-Leaders_2015.pdf

NSW Department of Education. (2022). Formal middle leadership in NSW public schools. Retrieved from https://education.nsw.gov.au/teaching-and-learning/school-leadership-institute/research/middle-leadership

Oleszewski, A., Shoho, A., & Barnett, B. (2012). The development of assistant principals: A literature review. *Journal of Educational Administration, 50*, 264–286. doi:10.1108/09578231211223301.

Oliver, R. (2005). Assistant principal professional growth and development: A matter that cannot be left to chance. *Educational Leadership and Administration, 17*, 89–100.

O'Leary, T. M. (2022). *Classroom vibe: Practical strategies for a better classroom culture.* Amba Press.

Peters, G., Gurley, D. K., Fifolt, M., Collins, L., & McNeese, R. (2016). Assistant principals' perceptions regarding the role and the effectiveness of an educational leadership program. *International Journal of Higher Education, 5*(1), 183–199.

Productivity Commission. (2022). *5 Year Productivity Inquiry: From learning to growth.* Retrieved from https://www.pc.gov.au/inquiries/current/productivity/interim5-learning

Professional Qualifications for Principals. Retrieved from https://www.unrwa.org/sites/default/files/adec_professional_standarda_for_principals.pdf. Accessed on 2 March 2022.

Reed, D. B., & Himmler, A. H. (1985). The work of the secondary assistant principalship: A field study. *Education and Urban Society, 18*(1), 59–84.

Rewarding Excellence in Teaching: Options paper. NSW Department of Education. Retrieved from https://education.nsw.gov.au/public-schools/rewarding-excellence-in-teaching#Release0.

Rice, J. (2010). *Principal effectiveness and leadership in an era of accountability: What research says.* Retrieved from http://www.urban.org/sites/default/files/publication/33341/1001370-Principal-Effectiveness-and-Leadership-in-an-Era-of-Accountability-What-Research-Says.PDF

Rossettie, C. (2022). *Who has seen the wind?* Poetry.com. STANDS4 LLC. Retrieved from https://www.poetry.com/poem/5987/who-has-seen-the-wind%3F. Accessed on 01 October 2022.

Scroggins, A. J., & Bishop, H. L. (November 1993). A review of the roles and responsibilities of assistant principals. Paper presented at the American Educational Research Association Annual Meeting, New Orleans.

Searby, L., Browne-Ferrigno, T., & Wang, C. (2017). Assistant principals: Their readiness as instructional leaders. *Leadership and Policy in Schools, 16*(3), 397–430.

Sherin, M. G., Jacobs, V. R., & Philipp, R. A. (2011). Situating the study of teacher noticing. In M. G. Sherin, V. R. Jacobs, & R. A. Philipp (Eds.), *Mathematics teacher noticing: Seeing through the teachers' eyes* (pp. 3–13). New York, NY: Routledge.

Southern Regional Education Board. (2007). *Good principals aren't born — They're mentored: Are we investing enough to get the school leaders we need?* Atlanta, GA: Author.

The Teacher Leaders Model Standards. (2020). Retrieved from https://www.nea.org/resource-library/teacher-leader-model-standards

Thích, Nhất Hạnh. (n.d.). *Quoteslyfe.com.* Retrieved from https://www.quoteslyfe.com/quote/You-cannot-transmit-wisdom-and-insight-to-920689. Accessed on 18 July 2022.

Thomson, S., & Hillman, K. (2020). *The teaching and learning international survey 2018. Australian report volume 2: Teachers and school leaders as valued professionals.* ACER.

Tschannen-Moran, M. (2014). *Trust matters: Leadership for successful schools* (2nd ed.). San Francisco, CA: Jossey-Bass.

Tschannen-Moran, M., & Gareis, C. R. (2004). Principals' sense of efficacy: Assessing a promising construct. *Journal of Educational Administration, 42*(5), 573–585.

Tschannen-Moran, M., & Gareis, C. R. (2007). Cultivating principals' sense of efficacy: What supports matter? *Journal of School Leadership, 17*, 89–114.

Tschannen-Moran, M., & Gareis, C. R. (2015). Faculty trust in the principal: An essential ingredient in high-performing schools. *Journal of Educational Administration, 53*, 66–92.

Turnbull, J., Riley, D., & MacFarlane, J. (2013). Building a stronger principalship.

In *Cultivating talent through a principal pipeline (Vol. 2)*. New York, NY: The Wallace Foundation.

Twain, M. (n.d.). *theysaidso.com*. Retrieved from https://theysaidso.com/quote/mark-twain-twenty-years-from-now-you-will-be-more-disappointed-by-the-things-tha. Accessed on 15 May 2022.

Villani, S. (2006). *Mentoring and induction programs that support new principals*. Thousand Oaks, CA: Corwin.

Wallace Foundation. (2007). *Getting principal mentoring right*. New York, NY: Author.

Wallace Foundation. (2012). *The making of the principal: Five lessons in leadership training*. New York, NY: Author.

Wallace Foundation. (2013). *The school principal as leader: Guiding schools to better teaching and learning*. New York, NY: Author.

Wallace Foundation. (2015). *Building principal pipelines — A strategy to strengthen education leadership*. New York, NY: The Wallace Foundation.

Weir, A. (2016). *The Martian: A novel* (First paperback classroom edition). New York, NY: Broadway Books.

Weller, L. D., & Weller, S. J. (2002). *The assistant principal: Essentials for effective school leadership*. Thousand Oaks, CA: Corwin.

Wood, R. E., & Bandura, A. (1989). Social cognitive theory of organizational management. *Academy of Management Review, 14*, 361–384.

Zierer, K. (2021). Effects of pandemic-related school closures on pupils' performance and learning in selected countries: A rapid review. *Education Sciences, 11*(6), 252.

Zimpher, N. L. (n.d.). *Quoteslyfe.com*. Retrieved from https://www.quoteslyfe.com/quote/We-make-no-apologies-for-setting-high-910116. Accessed on 18 May 2022.

INDEX

A

Active listening, 37–38, 38 (table), 107–108
Alberta Leader Quality Standard (LQS),
    110–111
Alberta Teachers' Association (ATA), 4, 27
AP. *See* Assistant principals (AP)
Assistant principals (AP), 2–4, 7, 34
    community and culture, 120–121
    growth and innovation, 121–122
    learning and engagement, 117–118
    resources and operations, 118–119
    self-efficacy, 110–111
Attitudes, 19, 23, 29, 39, 43, 50

B

Bandura, Albert, 9, 95

C

Calming, 40, 44–45, 97
Cautioning, 44, 97
Coates, Susan, 4
Colorful metaphors, 7
Communication, 9, 18, 28, 56, 58, 83–84
Communities of Practice/Professional
    Learning Communities, 30
Community, 23, 24, 25, 28, 34–35, 49, 58,
    72, 84, 91
Competencies, 17–20, 23, 26, 55, 77, 86–87,
    96
Counseling, 44, 97
COVID-19 pandemic, 26, 28, 102
Craight, Liliana, 25
Culminating activity, 125
Culture, 24, 28, 33–51, 58, 77, 88, 91, 96,
    99, 106, 108, 120
Culture for implementation, 10–11
    active listening, 37–38, 38 (table)
    assistant principals (AP), 34, 48, 49–50
    calm, 44–45
    community, 34
    definition, 35–36
    discern affective state, 42–43
    environment, feel of, 35–36
    leadership culture, 37, 37 (figure)
    leverage social persuasion, 43, 45
    scaffold, 44, 44 (figure)
    self-efficacy, 46, 48
    skill, 39–40
    tailor feedback, 45–46
    thrill, 42
    unpacking, 47
    will, 40
Cup-half-empty, 45
Cup-half-full, 45
Cusack, Tim, 42, 47, 48 (figure), 50,
    63, 110

D

Davies, Wayne, 94–95
Dispositions, 11, 17, 40, 43, 45, 50, 51, 55,
    107

E

Email, 28, 96
Engagement, 9, 23, 58, 63 (figure), 66
    (figure), 79, 89 (figure), 106
Experience template, levels of, 123

F

Fertile learning, 33

G

Great resignation, 2–3
Great retirement, 3
Great Teaching by Design, 6
Guided learning, 55
Gutierrez, Salvador, 25–26

H

Hattie, John, 6, 108

Head of School (HOS), 28

Human motivation, 9

I

Implementation, culture for, 10–11
    active listening, 37–38, 38 (table)
    assistant principals (AP), 34, 48, 49–50
    calm, 44–45
    community, 34
    definition, 35–36
    discern affective state, 42–43
    environment, feel of, 35–36
    leadership culture, 37, 37 (figure)
    leverage social persuasion, 43, 45
    scaffold, 44, 44 (figure)
    self-efficacy, 46, 48
    skill, 39–40
    tailor feedback, 45–46
    thrill, 42
    unpacking, 47
    will, 40
International School of Curitiba (ISC),
    28–29

J

John, Hattie, 108

L

Leadership, 68
    assistant principals (AP), 2–4, 7
    attributes, 8
    barriers to, 4–6
    conversations, 41
    great opt out, 3–4
    great resignation, 2–3
    growth and development, 7–9
    growth plan template, 125
    implementation, 7 (figure)
    personality, 41
    predictive inquiry, 14
    school leader preparation, roots of, 10–13,
        10 (figure)
    strengths, 41
Leadership standards, 10–11, 112
    from around the globe, 21 (figure)–22
        (figure)
    around the world, 20
    assistant principals (AP), 16
    basis for training, 19–20

common themes, 20
definition, 17–18
few standards at a time, 27
inform training, universal leadership
    standards to, 23–24, 24 (figure)
leadership meetings, standards as success
    criteria for, 27
mastery of, 29
monthly conversations, 26–27
research, 18
stewardship approach, 24–26
success criteria for, 27
Learning Policy Institute (LPI), 3
Levels of Experience Model, 55
Leverage social persuasion, 43–46

M

Mastery experiences, 12–13
    beginning not an end, 76–77
    capacity realization, 86
    disequilibrium, 80–81
    expert noticing, 83–85
    expert noticing, cautionary tale for, 85–86
    giving and receiving feedback, 82–83
    greater capacity, realizing, 86, 87 (figure)
    growth and innovation, 76
    learning and engagement, 76
    providing, 79–80
    recapping, 77–78
    research, 78–79
    Universal Leadership Standards (ULS), 76
Mentorship, 8, 68
Motivation, 9, 42, 80, 108
MTSS, 49

N

National Association of Secondary School
    Principals (NASSP), 3

P

Parent council (PTA), 60
Parent Teacher Associations (PTAs), 58
Physiological arousal, 42
Pipeline, 7
Planning guided leadership experiences, 11
    assistant principals, 72
    building collegial trust, 69–72
    community and culture, 66 (figure)
    community engagement, 66 (figure)
    growth and innovation, 54, 67
    guided leadership experiences, 73

leadership development and trust, 68

learning and engagement, 54, 63

mastery learning experiences, 58–59

professional learning opportunities, 64

progressions of experiences, 55–57

resources and operations, 54, 64

staffing, 65 (figure)

universal leadership standard (ULS), 54, 62–63

Principal leadership, 48

Principal Sense of Efficacy Scale (PSES), 47–48, 110–111

Principal succession planning, 3

Professional development (PD), 60, 61

Professional learning, 4

R

Relationship-building, 9

Rogers, Kenny, 108

S

Scaffold, 44, 44 (figure)

School community, 36

School councils, 58

School leader preparation, roots of, 10–13, 10 (figure)

School principalship, 8

Science, Technology, Engineering and Math (STEM), 59

Self-appraisal, 45

Self-efficacy, 9, 42–43, 46, 46 (figure), 48–49, 110–111

measuring, 46

Skills

culture for implementation, 39–40

feedback template for, 124

Social Cognitive Learning Theory (SCLT), 43

Social persuasion, 45

Stewardship

celebrating, 95–96

community, 88, 91 (figure)

community and culture, 23–25

culture, 88, 91 (figure)

growth, 88, 92 (figure)

growth and innovation, 23, 25

innovation, 88, 92 (figure)

learning and engagement:, 23–24

operations, 88, 90 (figure)

pathway, level 3 assistant principal onto, 97

reluctant leader forward, 98

resources, 88, 90 (figure)

resources and operations:, 23–24

stakeholder learning and engagement:, 88, 89 (figure)

Superintendent of Schools in Alberta, 4

T

Tailor feedback, 45–46

Thrill

culture for implementation, 42

feedback template for, 124

Training modules, 4

Transparent standards, 9

U

Universal leadership standards, 29

Universal Leadership Standards (ULS), 49–50, 62, 64, 90, 92, 112, 113

assistant principal capacity. *See* Assistant principal capacity

inventory, 113–117

W

Watney, Mark, 35

Westfield Valley Regional School (WVRS), 59–61

Will

culture for implementation, 40

feedback template for, 124

Winding tree-lined pathway, 8

Z

Zoom meetings, 28

A SAGE Publishing Company

Helping educators make the greatest impact

CORWIN HAS ONE MISSION: to enhance education through intentional professional learning.

We build long-term relationships with our authors, educators, clients, and associations who partner with us to develop and continuously improve the best evidence-based practices that establish and support lifelong learning.